THE TRIVIA LOVER'S GUIDE TO EVEN MORE OF THE WORLD

THE TRIVIA LOVER'S

GUIDE TO EVEN MORE OF THE

WORLD

GEOGRAPHY for the GLOBAL GENERATION

GARY FULLER

ROWMAN & LITTLEFIELD
Lanham · Boulder · New York · London

Published by Rowman & Littlefield
A wholly owned subsidary of The Rowman & Littlefield Publishing Group, Inc.
4501 Forbes Boulevard, Suite 200, Lanham, Maryland 20706
www.rowman.com

Unit A, Whitacre Mews, 26-34 Stannary Street, London SE11 4AB, United Kingdom

Distributed by NATIONAL BOOK NETWORK

British Library Cataloguing in Publication Information Available

Library of Congress Cataloging-in-Publication Data

Fuller, Gary, 1941–
    The trivia lover's guide to even more of the world : geography for the global generation / Gary Fuller.
        pages cm
    Includes index.
    ISBN 978-1-4422-3565-6 (pbk. : alk. paper) — ISBN 978-1-4422-3566-3 (electronic)
    1. Geography—Miscellanea. I. Title.   910
G131.F868 2015   FUL
910—dc23
                                                    2014039781

♾️™ The paper used in this publication meets the minimum requirements of American National Standard for Information Sciences—Permanence of Paper for Printed Library Materials, ANSI/NISO Z39.48-1992.

Printed in the United States of America

This book is dedicated to my wife of fifty years, Barbara, who has provided patient support, keen editing, eagle-eyed proofreading, wonderful photographs, and creative ideas throughout.

CONTENTS

MAPS

ACKNOWLEDGMENTS

I am grateful to all the members of my family for their support, suggestions, and tolerance. Thanks also go to Jim and Wilda Metzdorf, Bill and Claire Phillips, Fran and Larry Travers, Sandee Drake, Carole Martin, and Pat and Paul Reichenbacher (the first buyers of the *Trivia Lover's Guide to the World*).

INTRODUCTION

When I first began to study geography, the big question constantly debated by the faculty and my fellow graduate students was: "What is geography?" I thought this was quite peculiar. Those studying chemistry, mathematics, or history (which I had done) have a reasonably firm idea about what it is they're studying. Only geographers seemed confused. I assumed someday I'd be told what it was I was studying, but that never happened. As I gained some understanding of the scope of geography and what it offered those who were devoted to its study, it seemed obvious to me what geography was and why it should be such a vital part of school curricula. Unfortunately, I have yet to meet the geographer who agrees with me!

People acquire knowledge in order to survive. Of course survival means something quite different today than it did one hundred thousand years ago (getting a job versus killing a mammoth), but the principle remains unchanged. When humans moved out of their ancestral birthplace (almost certainly in Africa), they began a journey of survival that took them to an amazing array of challenging environments. Geography describes those travels and the interface between what nature had to offer and the knowledge and learning mankind developed in order to cope. As the journey continued, geography described and explained the languages, religions, customs, technologies, and forms of economy that emerged as groups of mankind found themselves in relative isolation from each other.

This "survival journey" lasted for millennia as mankind constantly moved and discovered new ways to deal with the natural environment. Not all these ideas were successful, and I suspect that none were "sustainable" in the sense that word is used by environmental activists today. Instead, new ideas and processes had to be continually developed if disaster were to be averted. Through much of this time, there was a great deal of natural environment and few of mankind. Nature gave us a lot of leeway: settle in a river valley where freshwater is abundant, build settlements, pollute the river, then move upstream, then pollute again, then move to another unpolluted river, and so on.

About one thousand years ago, the expansion of mankind's domain ended with the settlement of Hawaii, Iceland, and New Zealand. Then geography took on the task of identifying, describing, and analyzing new survival strategies that no longer involved expansion but rather the reunification of mankind. We didn't recognize this reunification for what it was. People from places distant to us often didn't look like us, talk like us, or (in general) behave like us. Therefore, they weren't us. It must be okay to take their land, enslave them, kill them . . . or (better idea!) make them more like us.

The number of languages and writing systems began to diminish. Religions tended to coalesce into a relatively few universal belief systems. The number and intensity of conflicts increased as the differences that mankind had developed over the millennia now confronted one another. Survival sometimes involved not seeking new areas to farm as in the days of expansion but abandoning rural habitats for urban places. While mankind will always be bound by nature's rules, survival in the reunification era seems to mean coping with the environment that mankind itself has created. Meanwhile, death rates declined, implying that mankind had some control over death and, hence, survival, but which, in turn, produced huge population increases that again threatened survival.

Indeed, each time we produce something to aid our survival, we learn that there's a "catch"—something that again threatens us: industry produces pollution; atomic energy produces nuclear waste; medical advances threaten us with overpopulation, depletion of social security, or side effects of drugs. Geography analyzes and describes this give-and-take game between mankind and the natural environment.

So, I see geography as the science that deals with human survival. I suppose that one can argue that medicine, public health, and military science also deal with survival, but only in very specific ways. Geography embraces the whole of our survival history and future.

Why this book? Professional geographers in the United States—and the American public in general—fully realize that the study of geography—this all-important science that details our past survival and points the way to the future—has either disappeared from our basic educational system or has become so diluted that it is practically useless. Over the past fifty years, several notable attempts have been made by different groups in different places to restore geography to the school curriculum. They have not been particularly successful. As I describe in this book, so many ideas and plans to "improve" or "develop" impoverished areas fail because the people developing the plans are too far removed from the reality of survival. Geography is impoverished in the United States, and we need to identify what is really needed for its survival.

Professional geographers speak to each other through their journals. Only the occasional geographer speaks to the general public. It is that public, and especially parents of schoolchildren, who need to be involved in the survival of geography.

This is meant to be a fun book, something both parents and middle-school children can enjoy. I have added some concepts from geography that at least hint at the scope and intellectual depth of the science. With this book, I have tried to reach an audience who can help the study of geography survive. The questions are trivia, but geography is not trivial! Please help it survive.

CHAPTER 1

GEOGRAPHIC IGNORANCE STILL PREVAILS

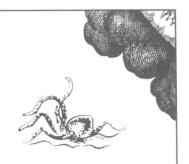

Question 1: What is the most active volcano in the world and where is it located?

Question 2: What volcano destroyed Pompeii?

Question 3: What is the smallest state in population?

Question 4: What is the most dangerous volcano?

Question 5: What is the only national capital near an active volcano?

Question 6: What do Milankovitch Cycles predict?

Question 7: In 1942, where did the Lost Squadron—consisting of six P-38s and two B-17s, which all ran out of fuel—crash-land and miraculously survive?

Soon after the publication of *The Trivia Lover's Guide to the World: Geography for the Lost and Found*, I became an optimist about people's knowledge of geography. Those I met on book signings and cruise-ship lectures were amazingly enthusiastic and knowledgeable. Geography is much better understood than I had thought. As time went by, I tended to forget about some of my undergraduate students, news reporters, and government officials, elected and appointed, who apparently

1

lived on Mars, or at least not on this planet. All this changed when I found some old boxes around the house.

What a mistake! I opened a packing box containing some of my mother's high school textbooks. They were old indeed since she graduated from Pulaski (NY) Academy in 1923. To my dismay, her geography text was more comprehensive, more detailed, more intellectually challenging, and, frankly, more interesting than any college-level text I'd ever seen. I guessed it was used in ninth grade, but I couldn't be sure. I was distraught over the realization of how our expectations for students have changed. Granted, some of the material in the old textbook was wrong and some was certainly politically incorrect by today's standards, but every page oozed challenges and excitement. Why do we expect so little today? Why have we watered down knowledge?

Isn't geography supposed to be the most exciting subject in school? Millions of people travel to volcanos and glaciers, major landformers studied by geographers. Kilauea, Pompeii, and the Juneau glacier field are among the earth's most fascinating places. The explorations of Magellan, Cook, Shackleton, Humboldt, and Wilkes rival the Apollo program and are more exciting than anything on *Star Trek*.

The majority of students entering my undergraduate courses were woefully ignorant of most anything to do with geography, including things in their own backyard (like Kilauea and Pearl Harbor). In part this was true, I think, because most of my students have lived all their lives in Hawaii. The system of describing common locations, a fundamental geographic principle, is different in Hawaii. Until fairly recently, the cardinal directions (north, south, east, and west) were hardly ever used. Instead, a local version of Cartesian coordinates was common. A place is either *mauka* (toward the mountains) or *makai* (toward the ocean) compared to another place. In Honolulu, a place may also be *diamondhead* or *ewa*, indicating direction along the coastline. This practice has changed in recent years since the interstate highway system built in Hawaii uses compass directions and because institutions like the University of Hawaii also use them (a West Oahu campus has been built).

Perhaps a different system of location means that maps are less common in Hawaii. Certainly ancient Polynesians sailed incredible distances across the Pacific and settled Hawaii without the kind of maps modern geographers use. Besides, Hawaii is the most isolated inhabited place in the world. In any event, while I had more than my fair share of brilliant students, almost 5 percent of my students could not locate the United States on an outline map of the world. Five percent may not sound like much, but consider the implications. If you're studying at a US university and live in the United States but don't know where your own country is, what has been going on in your earlier education? Is there much chance you know where any other country is? You may be thinking that those who couldn't find the United States on a map were foreign students, but you'd be wrong! Foreign students from any country can always find the United States on an outline map and invariably do better on map questions than American students in general.

A plumber cannot be overly troubled by raw sewage; neither can a geography professor worry excessively about geographic ignorance among his students. There were reasons to expect that things might get better. One national program, in existence toward the start of my career, the High School Geography Project, brought together new curriculum developments and intensive training for geography teachers. More recently, geographic alliances were formed between university and college geography departments and schools. If any of these programs has had any significant impact on geographic education, it has not been obvious. Congressmen don't know which of our states border foreign countries, one of Hawaii's senators implied that 97 percent of Greenland's glacier ice melted in July 2012, newscasters confuse Iraq and Iran, and a group of my students requested that I not ask any exam questions about glaciers since glaciers are not mentioned in the Bible.

It appears that my mother's geography class built a volcano out of papier-mâché, filled it with chemicals, and watched it erupt. Her textbook includes photos of volcanos from all over the world. There were also pictures of Pompeii, destroyed by the eruption of Vesuvius in AD 79. There was a picture of Mauna Loa on the island of Hawaii but none of its next door neighbor, Kilauea, which—while lacking the photogenic shields of Mauna Loa and Mauna Kea—is the world's most active volcano. How active is it? If I say it's always erupting, I am considerably more accurate than our senator is about Greenland!

What is the most dangerous volcano? That question would make an excellent thesis or dissertation for a geography student, but let me reduce the question to this: What volcano scares me the most? Unquestionably, Yellowstone. What? You didn't know that the majority of Yellowstone National Park is an enormous caldera with all that volcanic hot stuff close to the surface? Were it to erupt, it would be the largest eruption ever witnessed by man and would, I think, neutralize global warming. Yellowstone is estimated by one geologic study to erupt about every 360,000 years and last erupted about 360,000 years ago. As they say, do the math. Perhaps the folks in Wyoming, home to most of Yellowstone, have done their math, because it has become the smallest state in population size!

A number of countries have a plethora of active volcanos (including the United States, of course). Soils around volcanos can be highly fertile and the volcano, assuming it's high enough, provides freshwater from its runoff. Often overlooked, too, is the fact that the elevation of volcanos enables crops to grow that could not be grown in lowland locations. It's understandable, then, that farmers might take considerable risk to live on or near active volcanos. Certainly, however, no one would build a national capital on an active volcano.

As far as I know, only two countries ever did so. Martinique, now a *département* of France, built its capital, St. Pierre, on the edge of Mont Pelée. When the volcano went off in 1902, it killed everyone in the town except for a prisoner in a dungeon. This convinced the French to relocate the capital to Fort de France. That leaves only Ecuador, whose capital, Quito, wraps around Mount Pichincha. The eruption of 1999 left several inches of ash on the city, but the capital was otherwise unaffected and was not moved.

Dr. G. says: There is some hairsplitting over the number of survivors of Mont Pelée's eruption. One man on the edge of St. Pierre survived, as did a young girl in a rowboat. Compounding the tragedy, a second eruption occurred some days later, killing an additional two thousand rescue workers.

*   *   *

Mom's geography book also had a lot to say about glaciers, perhaps because she lived in an area profoundly affected by glacial advance, melting, and deposition. Over the past 750,000 years, continental glaciers have come and gone eight times. In North America, they covered most of Canada, New England, and parts of New York State and the upper Midwest. The last glacier episode, which ended about 11,800 years ago, is especially important because, as the glaciers retreated, mankind emerged as the dominant species on earth. Ironically, all the world's major religions, including those that don't believe in glaciers, were established during this period.

In general, glaciers have retreated over the past twelve millennia, but the overall process is complicated. During some periods and in some places, glaciers have actually advanced. The period from 1350 to 1850 is sometimes called the "Little Ice Age," and during this time, glaciers were observed to grow and advance, especially in New Zealand and Patagonia. For the past 150 years, however, many glaciers have substantially retreated and even disappeared. Alaska's maritime glaciers have mostly retreated miles up their embayments or fjords. Conversely, a few glaciers there have actually grown and blocked passages previously open to ships. Yes, retreat is the predominant theme, but please do not be influenced by guidebooks like one I bought that urges me "to visit Alaska quickly before the glaciers disappear." On the other hand, do rush to Kilimanjaro, where its glacier, located just about on the equator, is fast disappearing!

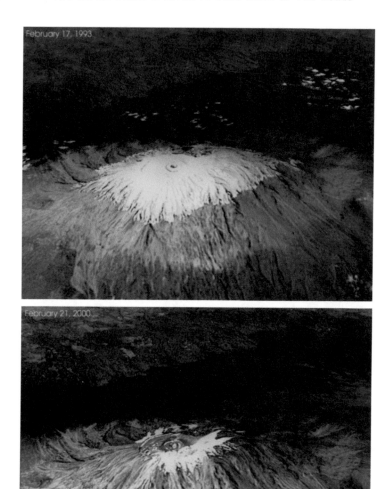

Mount Kilimanjaro glacial melt, 1993–2000. Source: *NASA.*

Will major glaciation ever return? Yes, in about three thousand years, according to the best estimate we have. During the First World War, a Serbian scientist determined that features of the earth's orbit and rotation changed cyclically. The earth's orbit, for example, changes periodically from being more round to being more elliptical and then back to being more round. These cycles, named after the man who discovered them, are called Milankovitch cycles. Strangely enough, they not only didn't appear in my mother's textbook, they didn't appear in any of mine either. Milankovitch cycles were rediscovered in 1976 and now are widely accepted as the cause of continental glaciation.

Before and during World War II, the United States ferried thousands of planes to Great Britain. In the days before jet engines and with altitude ceilings lower than today's, this was an incredibly dangerous undertaking and a lot of planes didn't make it. One notable example involved a formation of six P-38s and two B-17 Flying Fortresses that, in 1942, encountered a bad storm between Greenland and Iceland. After failed efforts to fly over, under, and around the storm, they turned around and headed for Greenland.

Greenland is covered with an ice sheet, a term that applies to glaciation exceeding fifty thousand square kilometers in area. While Greenland is constantly calving icebergs from its glaciers and therefore losing ice at its edges, the ice is more than ten thousand feet thick in the center of the island. The planes, collectively known as the Lost Squadron, did not have enough fuel to reach an airbase and crash-landed on the ice sheet. Miraculously, all the pilots and crew survived and were eventually rescued. The eight planes remained exactly where they had landed.

Fifty years later, an expedition was launched to find the planes of the Lost Squadron. One P-38 was recovered—from under more than 250 feet of glacier ice. This accumulation of ice in only fifty years provides an amazing contrast with the images that the press (and my senator) provides of a melting ice sheet.

Dr. G. says: Greenland's icebergs have caused much loss of life in the Atlantic, the 1912 sinking of the *Titanic* being the most famous example.

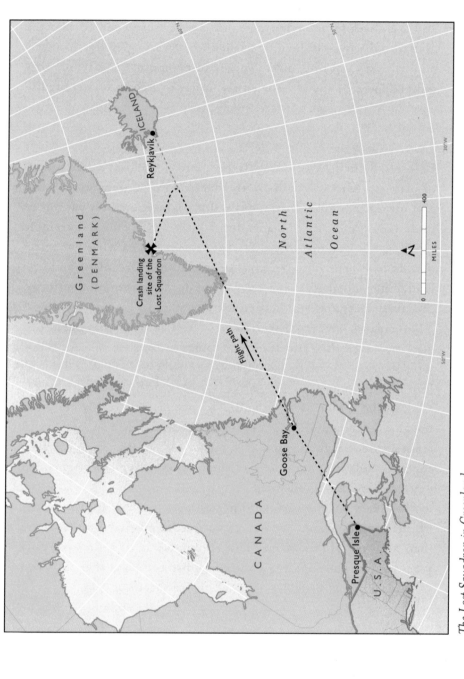

The Lost Squadron in Greenland

CHAPTER 2

WHY CAN MY STUDENTS FIND AUSTRALIA ON A MAP?

Question 8: What is the capital city of Australia?

Question 9: By what body of water did the Botany Bay colony settle?

Question 10: Who named the kangaroo?

Question 11: Where is the Fremantle Doctor?

Question 12: What feral animal, numbering in the hundreds of thousands, is being culled in Australia and its meat exported to the Middle East?

I taught geography to more than ten thousand university students during my thirty-five-year career. As I mentioned in chapter 1, almost 5 percent could not find the United States on an unlabeled map of the world. I realize that knowing where countries are is a fourth-grade skill and doesn't really belong in a college class, but how am I to teach geography—a science that connotes "whereness"—if my students do not know where things are in the world? Therefore, I added a simple map question to exams each semester so that students and I might at least have a common base from which to start. That's how I know about the 486 students who were clueless about the location of the country in which they were living and studying.

Strangely, only about 3 percent could not find Australia. This island country, with its continental proportion, stands out on a world map because of its size and isolation from elsewhere, thus enabling easy identification. By contrast, the main part of the United States, roughly the same size as Australia, is wedged between Mexico and that really large country to the north . . . what's it called again? My students' easy identification reveals a major aspect of Australia's geographic character: isolation. Its flora and fauna are unique in the world, a direct result of its isolation from other world areas. Its aboriginal people were quite unlike the native peoples Europeans found elsewhere. Even modern Australians stand out: like the third pig in the fairy tale, they like to build their houses with brick and mortar, they spend more time outdoors than most Europeans and Americans, and they seldom tip in restaurants, secure in the knowledge that the service staff receives a fair wage. Isolation is the key to understanding much about Australia. My students, in their geographic ignorance, accidentally uncovered an important geographic truth.

If finding Australia on a map is easy, anything else about it escaped many of my students. Because its settlement by people from Great Britain was so audacious and yet so successful, I would sometimes pose essay questions about it on exams. From the answers I learned that the first settlers were the von Trapp family, who crossed the mountains and founded the capital, Vienna (presumably singing "Waltzing Edelweiss"on the way), and about Captain Cook, who explored the area where the New South Whales live.

The *real* capital of Australia, Canberra, is one of the world's lesser-known capitals and ranks right up there with Tegucigalpa and Tbilisi for being hard to identify. This is a great pity, for Canberra is a wonderful capital. It features a new Parliament House (as well as the old one), wonderful museums, a world-class university, and a stunning embassy row. Perhaps you know that the US capital was designed by a Frenchman, Pierre Charles L'Enfant, but you are probably unaware that Canberra was designed by an American, Walter Burley Griffin. In 1911, Australia held a design contest for its capital city. Griffin's design was selected the following year from 137 entries.

Canberra, Australia

* * *

On my first visit to Canberra my hosts took me to a field just a few miles outside the city, where I stood virtually in the midst of a mob of kangaroos, the first I'd ever seen in the wild. To modern Australians, the kangaroo is a bit of a pest, but I suspect that the first settlers to see them had a reaction much like mine: I was awestruck.

The story, probably true, of how the kangaroo was so named reveals the severe problems the British—and colonizing Europeans in general—encountered as they ventured overseas. Captain James Cook in his barque, the *Endeavour*, discovered the east coast of Australia and went ashore at Botany Bay. He then sailed north and, in one of the greatest feats of navigation and piloting in the Age of Exploration, sailed the length of the Great Barrier Reef, eventually reaching the Dutch East Indies. The *Endeavour* did not escape unscathed but ran aground on a reef and had to be beached for repairs along the coast of today's Queensland.

Baby kangaroo (joey) as a family member. Source: *Queensland State Library.*

There, Cook encountered kangaroos and learned what the aboriginal people called them. He carried that information back to
England. When the First Fleet arrived at Botany Bay carrying the first
settlers from Great Britain, "kangaroo" was the one and only aboriginal animal name the settlers knew. The problem was that the native
people living around Botany Bay spoke a different language from
that of the people Cook met in Queensland. In fact, the Botany Bay
aborigines assumed "kangaroo" was an English word!

The tendency of European leaders to assume their colonial native
subjects were "all alike" eventually led to the emergence of independent countries in Asia and Africa that have been plagued since
independence with ethnic and tribal conflict. In the United States,
political and military leaders assumed that tribal governance of Amerindians resembled the systems by which American or European
countries were ruled. A treaty with, for example, a Comanche chief
bound only the chief and those in his band who agreed with the pro-

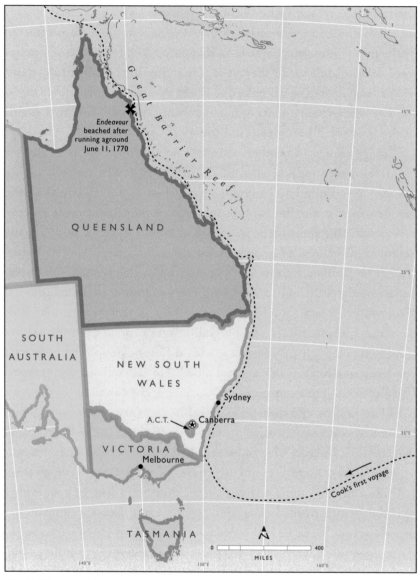

Cook's Voyage in Endeavour

visions of the treaty. Other Comanche bands, which US leaders may not have known even existed, did not consider themselves affected by the provisions. Just because Washington, DC, felt "all Comanches were alike" didn't mean they were. One side didn't fully understand what a treaty was; the other broke it whenever it was profitable to do so. The whole treaty-writing business was a disaster, one that is still in the process of being resolved today.

The ignorance in mother countries about their colonies calls for the development of a science of empire ruling. Why not call such a science "geography"? Geography flourished in the days when "the sun never set on the British Empire." How could Britain rule an empire containing territories as diverse as India, Nigeria, and Canada without the science of geography to describe, categorize, and analyze? The Roman Empire, in the days before university geography departments, still had to deal with the geography of its conquests. While Julius Caesar is seldom considered a geographer, notice how his famous commentary on the Gallic Wars begins. He tells us that Gaul is divided into three parts, with different people in each part (in other words, all Gauls are not alike). He also tells us the Belgians (Belgae) are not to be messed with because of the character of the land in which they live and their level of technology (preagricultural, living in swamps and heavy forests) and because they live so far from Rome that the Roman army cannot be supplied (distance, the sine qua non of geography). Caesar could not have employed his basic strategy ("divide and conquer") without a basic understanding of geography.

If the British needed geography to rule their overseas dominions, they also could be quite stubborn about it. Captain Cook's first landfall in Australia aboard the *Endeavour* was in a harbor that was originally named after the manta rays found there. Cook changed his mind, however, because of the botanical findings scientists aboard the *Endeavour* made and renamed it Botany Bay. When the First Fleet arrived, the passengers were charged with starting a colony at Botany Bay.

After attempting to live in the area, the settlers found Botany Bay lacked, among other things, an adequate supply of freshwater. They therefore pulled up stakes, sailed north, and entered one of the most ideal harbors in the world that, some years later, would be named Sydney Harbor. British colonial authorities, however, continued to call the settlement "Botany Bay."

Unlike Canada and the United States, which, in broad-brush terms, were settled from east to west, Australia was settled from the outside in. Coastal settlement ensured contact with ships coming from Great Britain. About fifty years after Botany Bay, Britain became concerned that the west coast of the continent would be seized and settled by the French. Accordingly, settlements were established in what today is the state of Western Australia, fully one-third of the country. Among the first settlements was the "Swan River Colony," which included what is now the capital of Western Australia, Perth, and an important port town, Fremantle. Relief from the hot desert winds in Fremantle comes with an early-afternoon cooling ocean breeze known as the Fremantle Doctor.

Was the Swan River named after the black swan, indigenous to southeast and southwest Australia? Quite likely, but geographers need to be aware of the Black Swan Theory, which, heretofore,

Australian black swan

economists have monopolized. A common expression in Europe, especially in Britain, before the discovery of Australia was that "something was as rare as a black swan." Black swans could not exist because all swans were white and always had been white. When black swans were discovered in Australia, it had a tremendous impact— much as if I discovered a flying pig. The philosopher John Stuart Mill succinctly defined the Black Swan Theory as the occurrence of something known to be "impossible" which then has a great impact on people and which people begin to rationalize by asserting that it should have been expected all along.

Gold and other minerals were found in Western Australia during the nineteenth century, and today they account for nearly half of all Australia's exports. Before mechanization, some means of transport was needed between Fremantle and the interior. Traditional European draft animals did not do well in the hot, dry climate, so camels were tried. Dromedaries were brought in from the Middle East, and some Bactrian camels from Mongolia were tried as well. After mechanization, the camels were no longer needed, and many were released. Conventional zoological thinking has it that dromedaries cannot survive in the wild and have become totally dependent on humans to provide water. Fortunately, the camels have not studied zoology. They flourished in the wild in Australia, and some estimates indicate that about one million feral camels now live in Australia and that their population continues to grow. Currently, they are being culled and their meat sold to Saudi Arabia.

Dr. G. says: Dromedaries have one hump; Bactrian camels have two. Camels, surprisingly, are native to North America.

PLACE NAMES: PRONUNCIATIONS AND TRANSLATIONS

Question 13: What is the correct pronunciation of the capital of American Samoa?

Question 14: What national capital can be translated as "fair winds"?

Question 15: What national capital means "red hero"?

Question 16: What country translates as "Black Mountain"?

Question 17: Where in the United States do we find a "classical name belt"?

Question 18: What is the more commonly used name for the country known as Aotearoa?

Place names can be baffling. The Germans were baffled during World War II when they intercepted and decoded a top-secret message that Churchill and Roosevelt were to hold a conference at the White House. Stalin declined to attend but the Germans hatched a plot to assassinate those at the conference. Unfortunately for German intelligence, the conference was actually held in January 1943 at Casablanca. The decoding was fine, but Casablanca translates from the Spanish as "White House." A coded message could be thus be decoded as either "Casablanca" or the "White House." Some earlier conferences had been held in Washington, so the mistake is easy to understand.

Try to explain to a foreign visitor why four of the boroughs that make up New York City (Manhattan, Brooklyn, Queens, and Staten Island) lack articles in their names, but we call the fifth "*the* Bronx." Further, New Mexico; Des Plaines, Illinois; and New Madrid, Missouri, are three places among many in the United States named after foreign places, but we pronounce them in ways people in those foreign places would consider strange indeed!

Place names are also dear to us. They are part of our identity. When we meet for the first time, information about where we are from usually follows our name. This is one of the main reasons why the failure to teach geography has so many bad consequences. I don't fully buy into the "low self-esteem" mantra of contemporary education, but I am convinced that students need to know how they are related to the landmarks of their lives, both people and places. Being lost in any sense of the word is a result of lack of knowledge: acquire the knowledge and esteem will follow.

We prefer that others properly pronounce place names that are important to us, and sometimes we are annoyed and offended when they don't. My neighborhood in Hawaii has a number of streets and landmarks that visitors have trouble pronouncing. In general, this is cause for amusement rather than annoyance. There are cases, however, when considerable umbrage can be taken. Once when I was teaching a class at Hickam Air Force Base, near Pearl Harbor, several of the students were members of flight crews who had been making practice bombing runs on an uninhabited island. What annoyed local members of the class was not so much the controversial bombing, but the fact that the Air Force seemed unable to pronounce the name of the island. Bomb if you must, but at least say it right.

Dr. G. says: The Hawaiian island then being bombed was Kahoolawe. The bombing has since stopped, and half-hearted attempts are under way to remove unexploded ordnance. Kahoolawe remains uninhabited.

Perhaps the most commonly mispronounced US place name is the main harbor and largest town in the only US territory south of the equator, American Samoa. The town and main harbor are named Pago Pago. The correct pronunciation is "Pango Pango," but rare is the American newscaster or even cruise-ship captain who includes the "n" sound. Actually, Samoan words in general that contain a "g" have an "n" sound before the "g." A noted University of Hawaii football player of Samoan ancestry had the surname "Noga." As you now know, his name was properly pronounced "Nonga." He and other Samoan athletes with the "g" in their names seem to have given up and accepted the American mispronunciation of their names.

> Dr. G. says: Pago Pago also provides a bonus trivia question. The StarKist tuna factory in the harbor calls itself the home of Charlie the Tuna, the star of numerous TV ads.

The story is told in Samoa that early printing presses lacked sufficient letters for their fonts. Thus, when it was noted that the "ng" sound appeared often in the Samoan language, it was expedient to use only the "g" to represent it. This story may be true, but experienced trivia players know to be skeptical about stories that so conveniently explain things. The association of "Ring around the Rosy" with bubonic plague is a classic example of a widely used explanation that is highly dubious.

Another American place name commonly mispronounced is Worcester, Massachusetts. It should be pronounced "Wooster," but many pronounce it "Wor-chester." What makes this even more confusing is that there is a city in Ohio, Wooster, pronounced just the way it looks!

* * *

Argentina is inaccurately named! The name comes from the Latin word *argentum*, meaning "silver." The river that borders it on the north is La Plata (The Platte), which means "silver" in Spanish. Despite the emphasis on silver, there is no silver in the valley or estuary of the Platte and very little in Argentina overall. The capital, Buenos Aires, is the second-largest city in South America. The city's name means "fair winds," and it is a major port.

Argentina and Buenos Aires were, and are, heavily dependent on international trade, but in the days when Spain ruled Argentina, trade was heavily affected by what might be called a distortion of distance. Economic geography stresses the role of distance in, for example, the location of manufacturing plants (affecting the cost of assembling raw materials and shipping finished products to market), the location of many service activities (how far will you travel for a Big Mac?), and even the crop choices farmers make. In colonial trade, Argentina would seem to be favorably positioned. Buenos Aires's location on the Platte gave it easy access to the Atlantic and hence to Spanish ports. Particularly in comparison with the Pacific coast countries of Chile and Peru, Argentina had easier access to Europe, especially before the Panama Canal was built.

In reality, colonial Argentina was unable to use the Atlantic as much as it would have liked. Its products took several routes to markets in Europe, but a common one was overland across the Andes to Valparaiso, then by ship to Lima, from there by land across Panama, and finally reloading on ships and departing for Spain either directly from Panama or from Cartagena, Colombia.

What forced this distortion of distance? Piracy was the main cause. It was no secret that ships sailing from the New World to Spain carried valuable cargoes, sometimes fantastically valuable ones. The pirates, moreover, were frequently highly capable sailors, often former members of the British Royal Navy. Even worse, Britain was frequently at war with Spain during the colonial era and brought to bear on Spanish treasure ships the world's largest and most capable navy. The Spanish attempted to defend themselves much like cargo ships crossing the Atlantic in WWII: through the use of convoys, which the Spanish called *flotas*. The idea was simple enough: many ships in a cluster could defend themselves better than individual ships. This did not work all that well because it was difficult for sailing ships to remain together, especially at night. Also (and this was true with World War II convoys as well) it was easier for pirates to find a group of ships than to find a single ship or two in the vast Atlantic.

Dr. G. says: Many pirates were not only good seamen but also good geographers. See more about their spatial strategies in chapter 17.

*   *   *

Mongolia conjures up images of caravans and vast yurt encampments, but its modern history dates to the 1920s, when it was invaded by a White Russian–Mongolian army that freed it from control by the Qing (Manchu) dynasty. Shortly thereafter it was invaded by a Red Russian–Mongolian army that eventually defeated the opposition force and established Mongolia as the second Communist country in the world (after, of course, the Soviet Union).

Its capital was renamed Ulan Bator ("red hero"). Ulan Bator has the distinction of being the world's coldest national capital. Temperatures range from about 60 degrees below zero (F) to 101 above. The city is located on the edge of the permafrost belt, which impedes

Dr. G. says: Here's another trivia bonus: the flag of Mongolia contains a mythical bird in Buddhist tradition, the Garuda. Garuda also happens to be the name of Indonesia's national airline. Indonesia is a Muslim country but has the same mythical bird in its traditions.

some modern construction, but in much of the suburban area yurts still predominate, so foundations are not required.

How did the Italians get to name so many places outside Italy? Sierra Leone ("lion mountain") was initially named by the Portuguese, not for mountain lions or for mountains where lions live but for a lion-shaped mountain overlooking what is now the capital, Freetown. But the name is not Portuguese—it's Italian! Why a country in West Africa should have an Italian name certainly puzzles me. On the Balkan Peninsula we find the country of Montenegro ("Black Mountain"), once part of Yugoslavia, then, along with Serbia, part of a new Yugoslavia, and finally, by the narrowest of votes by its citizenry, an independent country. Montenegro, too, is an Italian name! In this case, the word comes from Venetian Italian, used before a national, modern Italian language emerged.

Before leaving the Italian influence on place names, we should remind ourselves that North and South America are Italian names, as is (probably) anything named "Columbus." Were you to drive in New York State from Albany to Buffalo, you might encounter Rome, Syracuse, and Naples and think the Italians had struck again. Central New York, opened for settlement right after the American Revolution, assumed the spirit of the times. America viewed itself as a successor to classical culture . . . the glory of Greece and the grandeur of Rome. Houses built in central New York in the nineteenth century were often of Greek Revival style, and the place names included non-Italian classical names like Utica, Marathon, Macedon, and Ithaca. Bodies of water in the belt usually have Native American names, and there are a few British and exotic names as well. Unfortunately, so-called developers of suburbia in the area apparently didn't bother to learn about the geography of the area and imposed their Madison Avenue creativity on the landscape. Thus, traveling north from Syracuse, you'll encounter Euclid and Cicero but also Bayberry, named after a plant

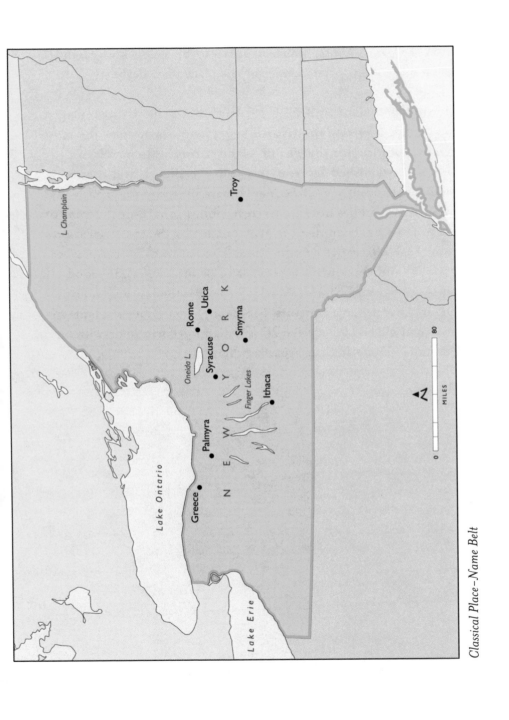

Classical Place–Name Belt

from the genus *Myrica*, which happens to be a Greek word and a much more appropriate name for the place than Bayberry.

My students could find New Zealand on a map. Unfortunately, they found it everywhere (North Greenland was perhaps the most creative location for this Pacific island nation). Modern New Zealand was established by treaty between the British and the native Maoris. In recent years, the Maoris have protested vigorously that the government has not kept its treaty obligations. One outcome of the protests has been that the Maori name for the country has now come back into more common use. The native name is Aotearoa, literally (and appropriately) the "land of the long white cloud." I put Aotearoa and New Zealand together on the last map question I ever gave my introductory geography class. One student approached me and asked what "this Italian word had to do with New Zealand." Those Italians are everywhere!

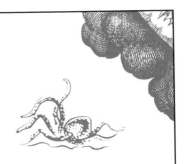

BORDERS AND
BOUNDARIES

Question 19: *What is the most frequently crossed international border in the world?*

Question 20: *What is the longest unfortified international border?*

Question 21: *What two countries does the Durand Line separate?*

Question 22: *What three countries are entirely surrounded by other countries?*

Question 23: *What is the andesite line?*

The Mexican-US border has drawn a lot of attention in recent years. At a Republican presidential candidate debate before the 2012 election, all the candidates agreed that their first priority, were they elected, would be to "seal" the border. It was not clear (to me) what "seal" actually meant. If it meant to prevent the illegal crossing of approximately five hundred thousand people per year (the rough average over the past decade), I am reasonably certain it can't be done. We have only to think of the Iron Curtain and how intensely the USSR and especially East Germany tried to stop people from crossing the border. Certainly their efforts were effective to a point, but the border was never "sealed"—and they were willing to shoot illegal crossers en masse, which we aren't.

Contributing to the difficulty of sealing the border is the fact that it is by far the most crossed international border, with about 350 million legal crossings annually. There are about forty-five crossing points between the United States and Mexico along a border that extends just under two thousand miles. One estimate claims that the United States has effective control over only about seven hundred miles of the border. Even with fences, electronic surveillance, and greatly increased numbers of border control personnel, the task of preventing illegal crossings is daunting. In addition to the facilities at the border, checkpoints have been constructed along roads leading from the border, usually a few miles inside the border. While the checkpoints are ostensibly aimed at controlling migration, their main function seems to have evolved into controlling contraband, especially illegal drugs.

Often overlooked in discussions about immigration to the United States from Mexico is the fact that a substantial portion of the United States was once part of Spain and Mexico. Spanish and Mexicans living in California, Texas, Arizona, New Mexico, and parts of other states at the time these territories were added to the United States didn't migrate: they were already here. Or, as Hispanic activists correctly note, such people did not cross the border; the border crossed them.

Nevertheless, one estimate is that one-fifth of all people now living in Mexico at one time lived in the United States, either legally or illegally. Additionally, thousands of Mexicans come to the United States legally for shopping. Parking lots surrounding the malls in Tucson, for example, commonly contain numerous cars from Sonora or other Mexican states. Estate sales and thrift shops in the border region often find that Mexican nationals are their biggest customers. Overloaded vans and trailers can be observed heading south toward the border on all major routes. In brief, "sealing" the border has far broader implications than might be presumed from the political rhetoric.

The War of 1812 is not the only "forgotten" war in American history, but it is the one whose outcome is the strangest. It's difficult to say who, if anyone, won the war or lost it, but all sides, the Indian-

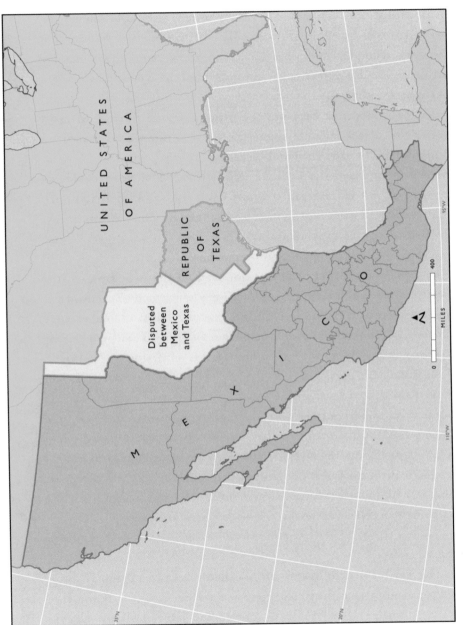

Mexico and Texas

British forces in Canada, the British themselves, and the Americans, were all satisfied with the outcome. The British burned Washington, the Americans burned what is now Toronto, and the Canadian forces repulsed major invasion attempts that the Americans thought were going to be easy.

In 1812, Great Britain was the only power in Europe to resist either the direct rule or strong political influence of Napoleon Bonaparte. The British navy blockaded French ports and, in turn, Napoleon imposed the Continental System, which forbade European countries and neutral nations from trading with Britain. To counter the Continental System both commercially and militarily, the British needed experienced sailors acutely. They stopped American ships at sea and impressed their seamen into the British navy. The British, moreover, had not honored all the provisions of the treaty ending the Revolutionary War. They continued to occupy forts on American soil in the Great Lakes region. Taken together, these things angered Americans and made them willing to consider waging a second war against the world's most powerful nation.

Regional feelings differed sharply. Henry Clay, congressman from Kentucky, led the "War Hawks," while New England, fearing occupation by forces from Canada, threatened to secede if war were declared. Many assumed that the "Tories," British loyalists who had fled to Canada during and after the Revolutionary War, would welcome an invasion from the United States. Once war was declared, much of Maine was occupied, and the Tories did not put out the welcome mat. Nevertheless, when a peace treaty was signed, although the war continued for some time afterward, all sides were happy with the outcome.

The period that followed, often called the Era of Good Feeling, led to an understanding that there was no need to fortify the US-Canada border. This almost changed when James Polk was elected US president in 1845. He campaigned on the slogan "Fifty-four Forty or Fight," the establishment of the West Coast border at a point that would have made Vancouver and Victoria (now in British Columbia, Canada) US cities. Once elected, Polk ignored his campaign slogan and instead carried out a promise he had made in the Democratic Party's nominating convention. He went to war with Mexico.

Today, the US-Canada border remains the longest unfortified border in the world, although it is more difficult to cross in either direction than it was only a few years ago and certainly more difficult than it was in the 1950s, when the border was highly porous. For some reason, Canadians visit the United States in great numbers during the winter months, strangely concentrating in areas like Yuma, Arizona, and several locales in Florida.

Most Americans have never heard of the Durand Line, yet in terms of American interests and foreign policy, it is one of the most important borders in the world. The Durand Line is the border between Afghanistan and Pakistan. It was established by the British during their rule in British India and is named after a British diplomat, Mortimer Durand.

The United States and its allies find themselves in a new kind of warfare in which the Durand Line is a pivotal issue. Geographically, this new warfare exists primarily in virtual space. Extremist Islamic groups, often operating with the tacit approval of less extreme Islamists, can launch an attack almost anywhere. When they do appear in real space, as the Taliban does in Afghanistan, the United States has the military power to destroy them—if only the Taliban would stand still and fight like armies used to do. Instead, they melt into the mountainous terrain that makes up most of the Durand Line and then cross into Pakistan. Pakistani forces either can't or are unwilling to do much about this. When US forces attack across the Durand Line, the Pakistani government becomes very upset.

Compounding this political reality is the religious reality of many Islamic leaders arguing that there shouldn't be boundaries between Muslim countries. This becomes even more understandable in the case of the Durand Line because both when it was established and now, it separates a group of people, the Pashtuns, whose herding and trading activities have largely ignored any border between Afghanistan and Pakistan.

Three countries are entirely swallowed up within the borders of another country: Lesotho, San Marino, and Vatican City. Lesotho is surrounded by South Africa, while San Marino and the Vatican are within the borders of Italy. Geographers like to refer to such entities as "enclaves," and most enclaves don't last long. San Marino, however, has been around since the fourth century, and the Vatican has an international following (the Roman Catholic Church) that is likely to support its independent status far into the future. Lesotho's economy is closely tied to South Africa's, but I am a bit skeptical that future governments of South Africa will continue to tolerate a sovereign nation within its midst. Unlike San Marino and Vatican City, Lesotho has some enticing natural resources, especially diamonds. One of its mines produces diamonds with the highest value per carat of any mine in the world.

Lesotho, aside from being landlocked, lays claim to being the country with the highest overall elevation in the world and thus the answer to a trivia question I have never heard asked. Its lowest point is more than 4,500 feet above sea level.

Dr. G. says: You may be tempted to think that Tibet should be the country with the highest overall elevation in the world. We don't even have to measure, however, since Tibet is not a country but a part of China.

*   *   *

The andesite line is a term from old geography books and probably should be replaced by modern plate tectonics theory, but it still

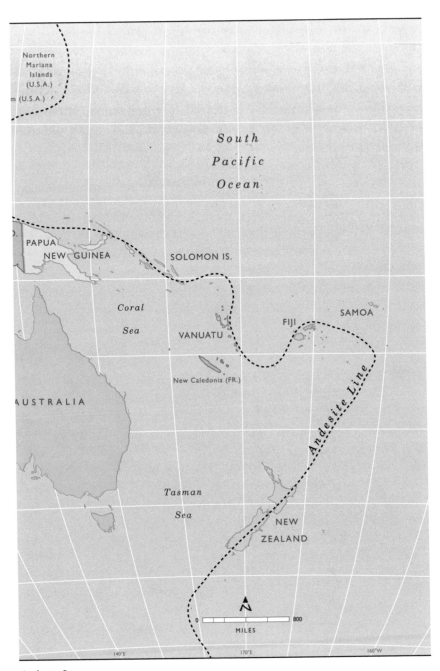

Andesite Line

appears on some contemporary maps, especially of New Zealand (where it was invented). The andesite line circles the Pacific basin and separates rock types. Outside the line are submerged continental rocks (andesitic), and inside it are the heavy basaltic rocks that characterize the Central Pacific. Paralleling the andesite line is the so-called Ring of Fire, an area of many earthquakes and explosive volcanic eruptions.

ISLANDS

Question 24: What is the better-known name for the Somers Isles (or Virgineda)?

Question 25: What US state is named for an island in the United Kingdom?

Question 26: What island group is named for St. Ursula?

Question 27: What island separates the Canadian falls from the American falls in the Niagara River?

Question 28: What are the second-largest islands in the Caribbean and in the Mediterranean?

The Spanish faced a real problem after Columbus opened the New World to them. Sailing across the Atlantic was one thing; navigating among thousands of islands and reefs in the Caribbean and along thousands of miles of new continental coastline was quite another. Going aground, even in good weather, and having the bottom ripped out of your ship was likely on every Spanish voyage of exploration. It even happened to Columbus when the *Santa Maria* went aground on the northern coast of what is today Haiti. Columbus had to abandon the ship along with twenty of her crew and return to Spain aboard the *Pinta*.

Spain tried a lifesaving scheme that sounds harebrained. The Spanish decided to put farm animals ashore on every island and coastline they encountered. The idea was that if marooned, Spanish sailors would be able to find food and survive until they were rescued. The plan worked in ways the Spanish could never have anticipated. The great longhorn cattle herds in Texas are direct descendants of Spanish cattle introduced there in the sixteenth century. The British colony at Jamestown also owes a debt of gratitude to Spanish foresight.

Jamestown, Virginia, was the first permanent British colony in the Americas, but it was barely successful and permanent only by charitable interpretation. The original colonists in 1607 were not farmers and seemed to have been on the verge of starvation soon after their arrival. Relief fleets from England attempted to resupply the colony, but even as they brought more food, they also brought more settlers to consume it.

Dr. G. says: Rather than a permanent settlement, we know the original Jamestown today only as an archeological site.

A fleet of supply ships attempting to reach Jamestown encountered a bad storm, probably a hurricane, and one of the ships ran aground on a group of small islands and reefs in the Atlantic, about six hundred miles east of North America. The ship, the *Sea Venture*, managed to land all its passengers and crew safely. Eventually, the survivors built two smaller ships from the wreckage and sailed to Jamestown, taking with them some of the pigs that abounded on the islands, descendants of the Spanish pigs left there decades earlier! The British named the islands the Somers Isles, after the captain of the expedition. Later, the islands were called Virgineda because of their connection with Jamestown. Today they're known as Bermuda.

Bermuda is one of the best fortified islands in the world. With an area of only about twenty-one square miles, Bermuda has more than ninety forts, most of them built centuries ago. While early British forts in North America were usually built of wood, Bermuda had no wood . . . but it had lots of limestone. The stone forts are therefore very well preserved.

TV and movies are so universally in color that we may forget that they originally were in black and white. Strangely, the situation with America's cattle herds is quite the opposite. Colorful dairy cows and beef cattle were once the rule; now, they're mostly black and white or all black. Of all the breeds and crossbreeds of cattle, my favorite has always been the Jersey. Smaller than most and often fawn colored, the Jersey is to cattle what the golden retriever is to dogdom. They are pretty and very docile.

The Jersey originated on the island of Jersey, one of the British Channel Islands. The islands are not part of the United Kingdom or the European Union. They are Crown colonies, owned by the

Jersey cow

British monarch, and are self-ruled under two administrative districts (bailiwicks), Jersey and Guernsey. They are a true political anomaly since they are part of the British Isles but not part of the United Kingdom.

Jersey was a strong Royalist supporter in the seventeenth century, and Charles II, who took refuge there, gave the bailiff of Jersey, George Carteret, a large tract of land in the New World. Carteret promptly named it New Jersey, thus giving us the only US state named after a British isle. Today Jersey's economy is heavily dependent on tourism, but it still maintains more than twenty herds of those beautiful cows.

Because the islands of the Caribbean were originally explored and claimed by the Spanish, it is not surprising that many were named after Catholic saints. In 1969, however, the Catholic Church examined its list of saints and decided that many were legendary, possibly real people but that they might have been based on pre-Christian traditions handed down to the present. Among these was St. Ursula, allegedly from Britain, who was martyred along with eleven thousand maiden attendants by invading Huns at Cologne, where Ursula was to be married. Aside from the scale of the wedding and the slaughter, the church was also dubious because it was impossible to provide even an approximate date for the event. Proposed dates ranged from the fourth to the ninth century.

Dr. G. says: The most famous saint to be "demoted" was St. Christopher, patron saint of travelers.

If Ursula has been removed from the list of saints, she still remains on the map. The Virgin Islands are named for St. Ursula, or at least for her martyred attendants. Today they are divided into the British and American Virgin Islands. A common trivia question whose answer always surprises contestants is: Who sold the Virgin Islands to the United States? The answer, of course, is Denmark.

Early in my career, I was engaged in a research project involving the attitudes of Asian students at the University of Hawaii toward different areas of the United States. Quite by chance (since it wasn't a focus of the project) I discovered that their favorite spot to visit in the United States was Niagara Falls. I was surprised, considering all the choices available. Niagara Falls is not particularly high as waterfalls go, although the amount of water carried over it makes it the most powerful waterfall in North America. Perhaps the most impressive thing about it is the vast amount of electricity it produces for both the United States and Canada.

Dr. G. says: The study showed, among other things, that if South Asian students were asked to choose anywhere in the United States to live, they highly favored agricultural states like Nebraska.

The Niagara River contains an island that turns Niagara Falls into three separate waterfalls: the American Falls, Horseshoe Falls, and Bridal Veil Falls. Somewhere in the midst of these cataracts—among the world's widest—is the US-Canada border. It was a well-established border in the nineteenth century, and the general agreement was that it ran through Horseshoe Falls. As the river has cut upstream, however, things have changed a bit so that the exact location of the border is now debatable. Quite possibly it runs right through the island that divides the falls: Goat Island.

The Mediterranean and Caribbean Seas are both noted for their islands, many of which are favored tourist destinations. The largest islands in each location are Sicily (Mediterranean) and Cuba (Caribbean), both of which, coincidentally, have been sources of significant migration streams to the United States. Both are large islands, but strangely, many underestimate the size of Cuba. It is the seventeenth-largest island in the world.

The second-largest islands in each sea are less familiar: Sardinia (Mediterranean) and Hispaniola (Caribbean). Sardinia had a long history even before it came under the rule of the Roman Empire. After Rome fell, Sardinia continued to be ruled by the Eastern Roman Empire at Constantinople and, later, Byzantium. Eventually, the Visigoths and Vandals took over, but they used much the same administrative system as the Romans. In modern times, Sardinia became part of Italy.

Hispaniola is shared by two countries: Haiti and the Dominican Republic. The tension between the two, which has always been high, is driven by a demographic and economic reality: Haiti is the poorest country in the Western Hemisphere and has one of the highest birthrates and greatest population densities. The Dominican Republic has a per capita income roughly six times higher than Haiti's and has perhaps the strongest economy in the Caribbean. The fear of Haitians storming the border, either as a mob or as an army, has long worried the government and people of the Dominican Republic, but, given their dependence on tourism, this potential danger has been played down in recent years.

Dr. G. says: During the Cuban missile crisis, Marine Commandant David M. Shoup opposed the invasion of Cuba and, at least according to legend, presented hawkish congressional leaders with a map. They were astonished since most thought of Cuba as being the size of Long Island. As Shoup had hoped, someone asked about the small red dot on the map. Shoup told them that the dot was Tarawa, a World War II US Marines objective that cost thousands of American casualties and seven invasion waves to capture. Quite likely, Shoup did not tell them he had won the Congressional Medal of Honor for his service at Tarawa.

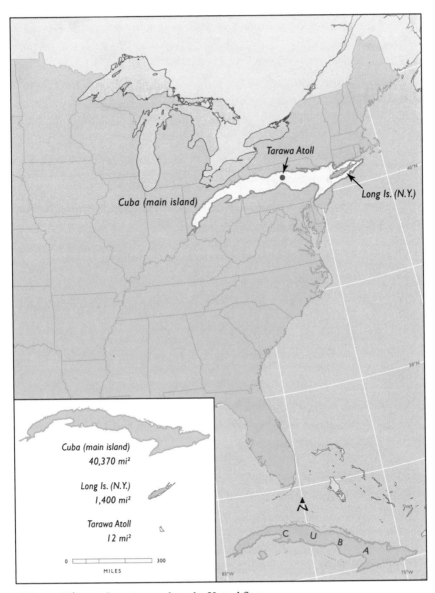

Cuba (main island)
40,370 mi²

Long Is. (N.Y.)
1,400 mi²

Tarawa Atoll
12 mi²

0 ⊏▭▭▭▭▭ 300
MILES

Cuba and Tarawa Superimposed on the United States

BATTLES

Question 29: Where was the battle of Lundy's Lane fought?

Question 30: One of Napoleon's greatest victories was at Austerlitz. In what current country is Austerlitz?

Question 31: Off the coast of what country was the battle of Trafalgar fought?

Question 32: One of baseball's most famous commissioners was named after a battle. What was the battle and where was it fought?

Question 33: What country would you visit to see the site of the Battle of Waterloo?

Question 34: Don Juan of Austria and Ali Pasha commanded opposing forces in what some consider to be the most important naval battle in history. Where was the battle fought?

Question 35: The turning point of World War II in Europe was said to be the battle of Stalingrad. What name did the Russians give to Stalingrad after the collapse of the Soviet Union?

Battles often seem to occur at random places. The location of Gettysburg, the turning-point battle of the US Civil War, was influenced in part by the need to find shoes for General Lee's army. Waterloo, a battle featuring British, French, and Prussian troops, occurred on a field foreign to all sides. We can usually find, however, that a great many geographic factors have coalesced to determine a battle site.

Let's place an American in a bar in Toronto, surrounded by Canadians, drinking Molson's, telling moose jokes, and spinning Newfie tales, when suddenly someone mentions the Battle of Lundy's Lane. The Canadians are smirking, but the American has no idea why. He's about to learn.

In the War of 1812, the War Hawks in Congress, led by Henry Clay of Kentucky, fully expected that many of those living in Upper Canada, expatriate Americans who had remained loyal to Britain during the American Revolution, would welcome an American invasion. The thinking was that these "Tories" would embrace the Americans, join with them, and get rid of British rule in all of North America. One of the places the invasion occurred was on the Niagara frontier, near Niagara Falls. This was where the Battle of Lundy's Lane took place.

Dr. G. says: In 1791, Britain created Upper and Lower Canada from settled territories around the Great Lakes and St. Lawrence River valley. Some Americans are confused by the names because they do not know how to properly read maps. "Upper" in this case does not mean north, but rather the upper reaches of the St. Lawrence, which flows from south to north. Actually, Upper Canada became the Province of Ontario (to which more was added later), and it lay to the southwest of Lower Canada.

The Americans were highly impressed with their own military operations at Lundy's Lane. The battle was then (and now) considered a tactical masterpiece by the American forces. Unfortunately, for several reasons, the Americans returned to the US side of the border, exactly what the Canadians were trying to accomplish. It was clearly a strategic victory for Canada.

The American should remind the smirking Canadians that, while Lundy's Lane slipped from his memory, he did recall that the

Americans made it to York and burned that city. That's the same city, Toronto, where the American is now smirking Yankee-style.

In December 1805, Napoleon Bonaparte marched his army, which had been assembled and trained in western France for an invasion of England, across the continent to engage an army of the Third Coalition east of Vienna. The coalition army was made up mainly of Austrian and Russian troops. The ensuing battle, about eight hours of sustained and bloody fighting, proved a decisive victory for the French. This battle was fought near Austerlitz in what is now the Czech Republic.

Napoleon's victory was of particular importance because it spelled the end of the Holy Roman Empire, an institution that began with Charlemagne in AD 800 (or, in the view of some historians, with Otto I in AD 962) and had been an important influence throughout Europe's medieval period.

Dr. G. says: One of Paris's most familiar landmarks, the Arc de Triomphe, was built to commemorate Napoleon's victory at Austerlitz.

While Paris went wild with the excitement of Napoleon's victory, London celebrated as well because, while the French won at Auster-litz, Horatio Nelson had earlier won one of the greatest sea victories in British history when he defeated a Franco-Spanish fleet at Tra-falgar, off the coast of Spain.

Napoleon's victory had involved magnificent battlefield tactics and a clear chain of command (which the Third Coalition lacked), while Nelson's victory had involved an unusual plan of attack that sacrificed central-command control for individual command and initiative by each of Nelson's captains.

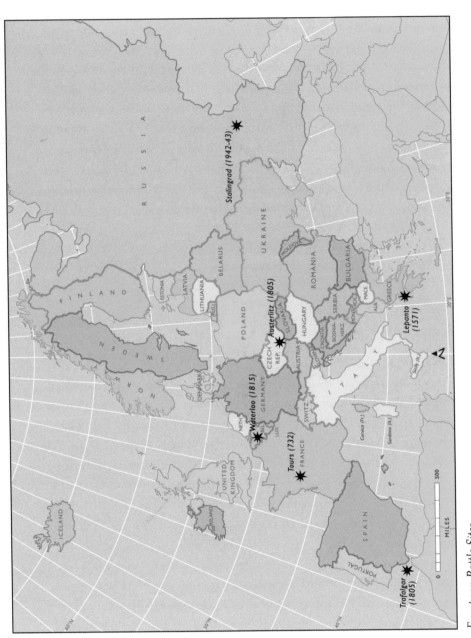

European Battle Sites

* * *

Many of us have "met our Waterloos," but the first to do so was, of course, Napoleon Bonaparte. Many of Napoleon's early battles had been fought by conscripts. He was the first to use the military draft on a major scale; while forced military service was an ancient concept, through much of European history wars had been fought primarily by professional soldiers. At his final battle, Napoleon did not use conscripts. His army, which he virtually recruited single-handedly, consisted of seasoned veterans.

Dr. G. says: Probably because of the draft, France after the Napoleonic Wars was the first to experience a postwar "baby boom."

Napoleon's chief enemies were the British and the Prussians, who, realizing that Napoleon (who was supposed to be banished to Elba) had raised an army, attempted to join forces. The British landed troops in the Netherlands and moved eastward, while Prussian troops raced westward to join with the British. Napoleon moved north to prevent their merger. The three forces met at Waterloo, then part of the Kingdom of the Netherlands but now in Belgium. Napoleon was defeated by the two armies (called the Eighth Coalition) and ended up banished on a more distant island, St. Helena, in the South Atlantic.

In the 1919 baseball World Series, professional gamblers bribed several members of the American League's Chicago White Sox to throw the series and allow the National League's Cincinnati Reds to win. No laws prohibited what had occurred, but several White Sox players were indicted on charges of defrauding an innocent White Sox player of the amount he would have received as a member of the win-

Dr. G. says: Johnston's tactics—avoiding direct battle with Sherman unless his own forces held a significant advantage (like his position on Kennesaw Mountain)—were optimal and brilliant. His replacement, General Hood, was quickly and decisively defeated by Sherman, who then seized Atlanta.

ning team. All the players were acquitted in court, but baseball owners were not satisfied with the verdict. They appointed baseball's first commissioner to investigate what was called the "Black Sox" scandal.

The man they appointed was a federal judge, Kennesaw Mountain Landis, named for a famous battle in the Civil War. At the time of the battle, Sherman's "March to the Sea" was well under way. His flanking movements had forced the retreat of Confederate general Joe Johnston, but the Confederates finally dug in on Kennesaw Mountain, just outside Atlanta, Georgia. After repulsing two assaults by Sherman's men, Johnston was threatened by an attack on his flank and was forced to retreat. Johnston was relieved of command because of the retreat.

Commissioner Landis banned from baseball all those even remotely involved with allowing Cincinnati to win. In a strange precursor to baseball's current "doping" scandals, Landis banned Shoeless Joe Jackson from the game. In the series, Joe had hit .365 with a home run, had committed no errors, and astoundingly had thrown five runners out from his left-field position. All those who had received bribes denied that Jackson had participated in the "fix" in any way. Shoeless Joe was considered by some to have been the greatest hitter to ever play the game.

For more than a thousand years, Islamic and Christian armies contended over territory in Europe. Muslims believed that it was the will of God that they spread their beliefs, whether through military conquests or less violent conversions. The first Islamic thrust into Europe began as early as the eighth century with intrusions into Spain. An epic battle in France, sometimes called the Battle of Tours, sometimes the Battle of Poitiers, was fought in AD 732 or 733. Charles Martel defeated the Muslims and apparently discouraged their further expansion in western Europe.

The fortunes of these early Islamic invaders, who were both Arabs and people conquered by the Arabs in North Africa, continued to wane until they were finally expelled from Spain in 1492, following the Spanish takeover of Granada. Just as this threat to Christian Europe was ending, another emerged in Asia Minor and eastern Europe.

The Ottoman Turks captured Constantinople in 1453, thus consolidating their rule over the former Byzantine Empire. Mostly Islamic, the Turks, like the Arabs before them, threatened to overrun Christian Europe. In 1571, the Turks besieged fortifications on Cyprus controlled by the Venetians. The Venetians surrendered under the agreement that they would be able to leave freely. The Turks, however, reneged on the agreement and executed the Venetian commanders. Meanwhile, Pope Pius V had created a Holy League, a coalition of southern European maritime powers, and placed its fleet under the command of a Hapsburg, Don Juan of Austria.

The Holy League fleet assembled in Messina, Sicily, and met a Turkish fleet leaving Lepanto. The Christians won an overwhelming victory, probably based on two decisive factors. The Venetian fleet carried cannons, while the Turks had only archers (but of outstanding ability). Further, the ships in both fleets were galleys, that is, they were propelled by oarsmen, but the Turkish rowers were slaves, while the Christian rowers were freemen. This made a real difference in the hand-to-hand fighting that characterized much of the battle.

Dr. G. says: This was the last major battle in world history to be fought by ships that were rowed.

The Ottomans rebuilt their fleet after Lepanto but eventually abandoned it. As time passed, Turkish military and naval power diminished while Christian Europe became stronger. For that reason, the battle of Lepanto is considered one of the most important naval encounters ever.

In June 1941, Hitler's Germany launched Operation Barbarossa, the invasion of the Soviet Union. German forces advanced steadily during the summer and revised their plans for 1942 to push the attack in the south so as to cut off the Volga River as a supply route. The city of Stalingrad on the banks of the Volga was simply a place on the map to the Germans. It is hard to overstate the importance of the battle that was eventually fought there from August 1942 until February 1943.

Stalingrad was the turning point of World War II in Europe. It was not merely a German defeat—it was the destruction of the entire German Sixth Army. The name "Stalingrad" took on significance for both sides as the battle developed. Stalin, of course, was the leader of the Soviet Union, despised by the Germans, respected and feared by the Russians.

In 1961, as part of the "destalinization" program of the Soviet Union, Stalingrad's name was changed to Volgograd. This was not a popular decision with the people of the city. The city government voted to change the name back to Stalingrad for six (nonconsecutive) days each year. They have also petitioned the Russian government for a permanent name change back to Stalingrad.

Dr. G. says: I know of no other city that has ever changed its name on selected dates during the year.

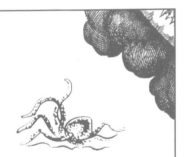

AIRPORTS

Question 36: Where did Lindbergh take off from and where did he land on his famous transatlantic flight?

Question 37: Where is Leonardo da Vinci Airport?

Question 38: What airport received its airport code designation because it was built in an apple orchard?

Question 39: Where is Dum Dum Airport?

Question 40: What is the world's busiest airport?

My personal greatest scientific discovery was that it is a waste of time arguing with the physics teacher about why a plane flies when the teacher is actually a phys ed teacher pressed into service. It is even *more* a waste of time to argue with all those textbooks that claim the Wright Brothers were the first to fly a heavier-than-air plane. Obviously, anyone who has made a paper airplane or a balsa wood glider has flown something heavier than air. What the Wright Brothers "Flyer" actually did was take off from the ground under its own power and return to the ground safely, precisely the requirements I insist upon from every airline I use. The sand dunes at Kitty Hawk, then, became the first airport.

Dr. G. says: Some texts modify the claim by saying the Wright Brothers made the "first controlled heavier-than-air flight," but that is just as nonsensical.

But if the phys ed teachers and the books have the Wright Brothers wrong, everybody else has Lindbergh and the *Spirit of St. Louis* wrong. Many think Charles Lindbergh was the first to fly across the Atlantic in 1927. Actually, the first plane to make a transatlantic flight took nearly a month in 1919, and because it was a seaplane, it could land and refuel at ships that were strung out like a picket fence across the Atlantic. Lindbergh was the first to fly solo, and he was the first to fly from North America to Europe; earlier transatlantic flights had landed in Ireland or Britain. Lindbergh started at Roosevelt Field on Long Island and landed at Le Bourget Airport in Paris.

Leonardo da Vinci was, of course, a geographer whose cartography was amazingly accurate for its day. Like many geographers, he was multitalented and dabbled in both art and engineering. He was particularly fascinated with flight and designed fixed-wing aircraft as

Charles Lindbergh and the Spirit of St. Louis

well as what may have been the first attempt at a helicopter. He also designed a parachute that has been built and tested in modern times but, because of its small air-holding capacity, was not particularly effective. Given the extent of Leonardo's talent, one might think the whole country should be named after him, but the Italians instead chose to name the airport that serves the capital after him. Leonardo da Vinci Airport is in the Rome metropolitan area.

Although some of my students had actually heard of World War II, their knowledge was a bit superficial. My personal knowledge of the war is also quite limited since I was born less than two months before the United States formally entered the conflict. Airplanes were a big part of my memory. Bombers (ours!) flew over my house in such great numbers that they exceeded my ability to count them. Bedtime came every night just as the nearby Franklin air-cooled engine factory began to test its engines; the roar lulled me to sleep. Air bases were built all over the country, and our family's driveway became a testing ground for concrete used in runways at the bases. While others in our neighborhood had gravel or dirt driveways, ours was nine inches of concrete.

On the northwest edge of Chicago, the Douglas Company had a huge facility to build some of the planes that flew over my house on their way to Europe. At war's end, Douglas decided to move to the West Coast, and the Chicago facility became an airport. On the site was an existing airport called Orchard Park, apparently because there had once been an apple orchard there. The new airport inherited the airport code for the old airport: ORD. ORD eventually became O'Hare, named after a World War II hero. By 1994, ORD had become the world's largest airport, handling far too many flights in the view of aviation experts. Today it ranks as the second-busiest airport in the United States.

The first time I heard Dum Dum Airport come up in a trivia game, one of the players insisted that it had to be the airport where US congressmen landed in Washington, DC. This was precisely what Mark Twain would have said in the nineteenth century and Will Rogers in the twentieth had the airport been around then; Americans' opinion of Congress has not changed much! In reality, Dum Dum Airport serves Calcutta, India. Indians know full well the implications of the name and prefer to call it something else. They also prefer "Kolkata" to "Calcutta." And yes, there is a Dum Dum school, several in fact.

Dr. G. says: Rather than for its airport, Dum Dum is better known for its bullet, developed by the British at the Dum Dum armory. The dumdum round is a hollow bullet that expands on contact. It produces devastating wounds and is outlawed for use in combat by international law.

* * *

Connectivity has long been a major focus of geography: transportation nodes, flows between those nodes, connectivity matrixes are all examined to better understand how the world is knit together. Airplanes and airports greatly increased connectivity, at least on a grand scale, and thereby increased the amount of interaction among people and places. Still, air travel sometimes has actually decreased connectivity by increasing travel time between certain sets of places. London and Paris are often given as examples since it is considerably faster to travel from central London to central Paris by train than by plane: travel time to and from the airports offsets the greater speed of the airplane.

Airports have also been overwhelmed by the number of passengers so that bottlenecks form at certain junctures. I have missed two flights while waiting more than two hours in check-in lines, but the most annoying delays occur when you miss a connection because the plane you arrived in can't get into a gate. The busiest airport in the world may surprise you—it is neither Heathrow nor O'Hare but Hartsfield-Jackson Atlanta Airport.

THE BRITISH EMPIRE

Question 41: What was the first British overseas colony?

Question 42: To what area in the British Empire did the Latin word peccavi *refer?*

Question 43: Where are the Plains of Abraham?

Question 44: Which two British possessions are claimed, respectively, by Argentina and Spain?

Question 45: What British possession, its oldest existing overseas colony and formerly a naval base, has virtually no freshwater supply, no significant industry, and the third-highest income in the world?

Question 46: What is the source of the (White) Nile River, and who discovered it?

An absolutely required course for anyone pursuing an advanced degree in geography used to be "History of Geographic Thought" or something with a similar title. Gradually this has faded away and, indeed, the tendency in the discipline has been to abandon anything with "history" in its title. When such a course was offered, it usually stressed the contributions, especially the theoretical work, of German geographers. Lacking this perspective, geographers now seem to have trouble building new knowledge on old. Chemistry and physics, for example, have placed one building block on another for centuries and thereby reached their current level of understanding. Geography's building blocks resemble a child's playroom after a temper tantrum; if one block remains on another, it is strictly by chance.

The British built their geography of empire one block on another for more than four centuries. The finished empire was the largest ever built, and the accumulated geographic knowledge was immense . . . much of it still untapped. As with most empires, military power built the early part and held it together. Captain Cook, the greatest geographer and explorer of his time, sailed for the Royal Navy. After Cook's death, however, the Royal Geographic Society (originally the London Geographical Society) took over. Sir Roderick Murchison, the head of the RGS in its heyday, has more than twenty topographic features named after him by explorers the RGS funded.

How did the empire start? It started in the reign of Henry VII and only five years after Columbus. A Venetian citizen, known in England as John Cabot, set forth from Bristol and was the first European since the Vikings to discover the North American continent. Cabot did not return with gold, Indians, or plants like Columbus did, but with a knowledge of a resource whose abundance was almost beyond imagination. We're not entirely sure where Cabot went or what happened to him subsequently, but the one (perhaps legendary) account of his voyage that had a real impact was this: Cabot and his crew found fish in such abundance that to catch them, it was necessary only to lower a basket over the side of the ship and haul in huge codfish. Later voyages reported that the fish were so abundant that if a boat were lowered over the side, the sheer number of fish made it impossible to row.

Cabot's discovery thus became Britain's first overseas colony, a "new found land" whose ocean treasures were the real prize. Newfoundland did not become part of Canada until 1949 and then only by a close vote of the population.

Before we leave the subject of cod entirely, it is hard to understand why the Pilgrims, initially on Cape Cod (note the name), largely ignored the marine resources that surrounded them. Not only cod and other fish, but also lobster and shellfish abounded along the coast of Massachusetts. What we eat is so bound up in our cultural traditions that we will literally starve to death rather than eat unfamiliar things—and the Pilgrims are probably an example. In fairness,

I should add that historians differ in their interpretation of Pilgrims and marine resources. The original accounts, however, only occasionally mention fish, and there is some evidence that the Pilgrims simply did not know how to fish.

The cod ran out in Newfoundland in the 1990s, and there are fewer people living in Newfoundland today than there were in 1970. The fishermen keep saying, "The cod will come back," and maybe they will. More than twenty years later, however, after a moratorium on cod fishing was declared by the Canadian government, it's still not certain that the cod will return to levels where major commercial fishing would be possible.

Dr. G. says: In Newfoundland, the island's name is usually pronounced as "New Found Land" rather than with the parts slurred together as outsiders do.

* * *

India was, no doubt, the jewel in the crown of the British Empire. It came under British domination piece by piece, and the complexity of Indian culture combined with the tangled relationships the British had with local rulers produced a colonial situation so confusing that it is hard to understand even when portrayed in broad brushstrokes. In truth, India is a British creation, an illusory unity created by colonial domination of many different peoples speaking hundreds of different languages.

The British army played a big role not only in protecting British mercantile interests but in keeping a measure of peace among people who had been enemies for generations. In 1842, General Sir Charles Napier was commander of all British troops in India. He was ordered to put down a rebellion of Muslims in Sind Province, in the delta region of the Indus River (now part of Pakistan). Some of the Muslims in Sind had supported the Afghanis in the First Anglo-Afghan War. Napier not only put down the rebellion but conquered all of Sind and brought it into the empire. According to a popular legend, Napier sent a single-word message to London: "Peccavi." This Latin word translates as "I have sinned," a pun on the statement "I have Sind." Like a great many stories, this may not be true, and I include it here because the legend has overtaken the truth and yielded one of the great pieces of (faux?) geographic trivia.

One of the most important battles the British fought as they expanded their empire was truly surprising because it involved relatively few soldiers and lasted less than half an hour. The British were contending with the French over the control of the St. Lawrence River, specifically the French fortifications at Quebec and Montreal. In the spring and summer of 1759, British General James Wolfe, with fewer than ten thousand troops but supported by more than forty ships from the Royal Navy, was attempting to take Quebec City. In preparation for the operation, James Cook, the great geographer and explorer, mapped the St. Lawrence and its shorelines. Although it might have been possible for the British to have besieged Quebec indefinitely, it seemed impossible to take the French stronghold by force . . . yet that's exactly what happened.

General Wolfe landed his troops upriver from Quebec and drew French General Louis-Joseph de Montcalm's troops out onto a plateau area above the river that had formerly been the farm of a man named Abraham. Hence, the battle of Quebec in 1759 is also called the Battle of the Plains of Abraham. The British routed the French and took Quebec.

Dr. G. says: Such a siege is dubious if one considers the Canadian winter. British ships would have been blockaded by ice at the mouth of the St. Lawrence and possibly even frozen in place.

*   *   *

It is ironic that the British Empire, built in significant part by the Royal Geographic Society, is now criticized in geographical journals and books, but it's hard to conquer most of the world without stepping on a few toes! In recent decades, significant objections have been raised to the British occupation of the Falkland Islands and Gibraltar: Argentina wants the Falklands (which it calls the Malvinas), and Spain wants Gibraltar.

Argentina's ruling generals decided to take the Falklands by force in 1982, apparently as a matter of national honor: the islands have fewer than three thousand people, a lot of sheep with high-quality wool, and little else. The generals apparently did not notice that Margaret Thatcher was prime minister of the United Kingdom at the time. Defending the islands from the Argentines would have been difficult enough, but retaking it seemed an act of madness. Thatcher reasoned that Britain must have a navy for a reason and so she ordered what might turn out to be the last surface naval battle in history. Yes, the British took back the islands, and they remain British possessions today.

I was in Washington, DC, shortly after this event, and it seemed that virtually everyone in the US government was asking, "Where in the world are the Falkland Islands?" Few knew.

Gibraltar is, of course, a huge rock that is becoming a significant tourist and retirement site. The British living there seem embattled; the British Union Jack is draped from a number of apartment windows. Two referenda held in recent decades have rejected Spanish rule over the tiny territory. On my first visit to a restaurant in Gibraltar, the people sitting next to us were conversing in what I thought was Spanish when suddenly a string of British-accented English entered the conversation, punctuated by a few words that seemed to belong to neither language. This was the first occasion I had to hear Llanito, a common language in Gibraltar. It makes a good trivia question!

* * *

The British Empire lost thirteen of its more promising colonies in 1776 and subsequent events, but it might well have lost a fourteenth. As described in chapter 5, Bermuda was originally an offshoot of Jamestown, Virginia. It was sufficiently far out in the Atlantic, however, that the Royal Navy ensured its loyalty to the Crown. Unlike Virginia, Bermuda could not successfully grow tobacco. While it did successfully build ships and yachts for a time, that industry faded, as did salt making, a commodity the British needed for their cod.

Eventually, the British Empire decided Bermuda would simply be a naval base and, indeed, it became a formidable one. Fortifications surround Bermuda, and what could not be protected by cannons could be defended by the coral reef that surrounds the colony. Antisubmarine warfare in the Atlantic during both world wars turned Bermuda into one of the largest and most important naval bases in the world. Eventually, the base closed down and Bermuda was left with a reputation for seasonal tourism and golf.

Adding to the problem of economic development was that Bermuda had no potable groundwater. Houses were built around cisterns, and whitewashed roofs were used to collect rainwater.

Bermuda rain-gathering system (rooftop)

The houses themselves were built of limestone blocks that offered security from the hurricanes that frequented the area. All in all, Bermuda seemed like an economic disaster in the making. Instead, its reinsurance and banking industries have turned Bermuda into the place with the third-highest per capita income in the world (after Qatar and Liechtenstein).

The British Empire had a recurring relationship with the Nile River. Nelson won an important naval victory there in the Napoleonic Wars, General Charles Gordon was killed upriver at Khartoum, and while the British government opposed the Suez Canal, Britain wanted control of it after it was built. More than anything else about the Nile, however, the nineteenth-century world and especially the Royal Geographic Society wanted to know where the Nile started.

The source of the Nile had puzzled the ancients as well because the Nile was unlike any other river in the known world. Geographers call the Nile an "exotic stream," which is another way of saying it flows across the world's largest desert, and during its course through Egypt, it lacks tributaries until the Blue and White Nile Rivers meet in Khartoum, Sudan. Perhaps most astounding of all, it floods just after the hottest and driest season in Egypt. Where in the world does all that water come from?

> Dr. G. says: A seasonal tributary flows from Ethiopia and enters the White Nile about three hundred miles upstream from the outflow at the Mediterranean, but it adds only a minute amount to the total flow.

Many, many explorers tried to follow the Nile upstream to find the source. None succeeded. An RGS-sponsored expedition in 1855 featured geographic explorers John Speke and Richard Burton, who attempted to find the Nile's source by going inland from East Af-

Source of the Nile

rica. They had scarcely left the coast when they were kidnapped and barely escaped with their lives. They tried again two years later. After months of trekking they separated, with Speke going north, where he discovered a huge lake which he named after the Queen, Victoria. Speke announced this as the source of the Nile. Burton was astonished and argued that Speke had not circled the lake to see whether it had a stream feeding it. Burton maintained that Lake Tanganyika fed Lake Victoria and was actually the source.

The Royal Geographic Society commissioned the most famous of African explorers, Dr. David Livingstone, to determine who was right. Livingstone's attempt is perhaps the most famous in the history of exploring, but he did not find the source of the Nile. Who did, and where is it? Actually, it may not have been found yet. It has been narrowed down to a mountain stream in Burundi, and satellite imagery has helped, but I still have my doubts.

MISSIONARIES: AGENTS OF GEOGRAPHICAL CHANGE

Question 47: What was the first religion to use missionaries?

Question 48: What missionary founded the first European settlement in Michigan?

Question 49: How many missions did the Spanish found in California?

Question 50: Who were the Saints of Kalaupapa?

Question 51: In what contemporary African country did Albert Schweitzer serve as a medical missionary?

In college and graduate school, I took all the courses I could that dealt with Latin America. In some of those courses, missionaries were never mentioned; in others, they were portrayed as a minor part of the Spanish and Portuguese conquest and administration. While I initially accepted that missionaries played a minor role in colonization, I eventually realized that the missionaries, rather than the explorers and soldiers, were really the ones who did the effective colonizing. Please note that "effective" does not imply a value judgment about the missionaries and the work they did. I mean simply that they had a more direct and lasting impact on Latin American peoples than any other group. Missionaries also did important things in Canada and the United States, but Eu-

61

ropeans settled there in great numbers. The cultures of those two countries resulted mostly from the settlement of Europeans, while in most of mainland Latin America what emerged was a culture of native inhabitants transformed by contact with Europeans. I saw the missionaries as the agents of the incredible change that occurred in much of Middle and South America.

So I waited for an applicant to our PhD program who would have an interest in studying missionaries as spatial change agents. Finally, one applied. He was keen on looking at how missionaries brought small-scale economic change in Asia. Unfortunately, his academic record was a long way from what we required for admission. I remained disappointed.

For most of mankind's existence, religious beliefs were one factor that united a small group of people and distinguished them from another small group. Aspects of one village's religion were sometimes shared among other groups and sometimes forced on one group by another. The idea of spreading a religion widely, however—proselytizing—appears to be something relatively new. Three of the world's major religions, Buddhism, Christianity, and Islam, are examples of religions that have actively sought converts.

Buddhism was the first. In the first three centuries BC, Buddhism spread from its origin in northern India throughout the subcontinent and into Ceylon (modern Sri Lanka). Following trade routes, it moved into East Asia, Southeast Asia, Tibet, and Mongolia. Over the next six hundred years, it disappeared from most of India. Because Buddhism is based on the Four Noble Truths rather than on a specific formula for worship, it was easily amalgamated with other religious beliefs.

Christianity is the religion most often associated with missionaries. Early Christian missionaries did their best to build a new religion on top of existing religious beliefs. For example, since the specific timing of Christ's birth was unknown, it is not surprising that Christmas was scheduled to "replace" the Roman Saturnalia, a big

Dr. G. says: In languages other than English, Easter is denoted by some form of the word "Pascha," which comes from the Aramaic (a form of Hebrew), meaning "Passover."

feast held right after the autumnal solstice. Similarly, the word "Easter" came from the name of an Anglo-Saxon goddess.

The year 1534 proved to be an important one in the largest missionary task ever undertaken by a single country: the spread of Christianity in Latin America by Spain. In that year, Cortez, the conqueror of the Aztecs in Mexico, requested that additional Franciscan missionaries be sent to Mexico; according to some sources, twelve Franciscans had originally accompanied Cortez. In that same year, Ignatius of Loyola, a former Spanish soldier, formed a religious community that came to be called the Jesuits. The Jesuits emerged as a particularly important link in Spain's missionary activity, but they protected Native Americans from enslavement and, in a number of ways, thwarted Spain's plans for the New World.

The Jesuits were active in the United States and Canada as well. The first exploration of the Mississippi River was by Father Jacques Marquette and Louis Joliet; Marquette was a French Jesuit who went on to found the first settlement in Michigan, at Sault Ste. Marie.

Dr. G. says: In 1534, according to tradition, the Virgin Mary appeared to an Aztec-speaking Indian outside Mexico City. While there are disputes over the events that occurred, an Indian cloak, or *tilma*, bearing the image of the Virgin of Guadalupe has become the unifying symbol of Mexico. The *tilma* portrays Mary as an Indian, thereby providing impetus for mass conversion. It hangs at the Basilica of Our Lady of Guadalupe in Mexico City. The place-name Guadalupe comes from Spain, not Mexico, and means "Wolf River."

* * *

In 1767, Spain expelled the Jesuits from their New World missions. At about the same time, plans were under way for the last major expansion of Spain's missionary network into Alta California. The Jesuits were originally supposed to build these missions, but the Franciscans took on the job. Twenty-one missions were built, from San Diego to north of San Francisco. A twenty-second was authorized for Santa Rosa but never built.

> Dr. G. says: Alta California was an immense area stretching inland, but the missions were situated near the Pacific coast, so in actuality all the missions were in the modern state of California.

The Spanish missions in California and Arizona dealt with an Amerindian population that was either preagricultural or, at best, primitive agriculturalist. Prior to the missions, survival had always meant the need to migrate with the available food supply. The priests, however, found it difficult to attempt religious conversion with a mobile population. The migratory behavior that had been traditional—and necessary for survival—was called "vagabondism" by the priests and labeled as a serious sin. Instead, the missionaries taught sedentary crop agriculture and ranching, and it was highly successful. The missions proved able to feed not only their own residents but the military at nearby presidios as well. By 1800, the missions in California showed an inventory of over one hundred thousand head of cattle; there had, of course, been no cattle (an animal not native to the New World) in California prior to the arrival of the Spanish.

When independence came to Mexico, the Spanish missions collapsed and, initially at least, the church lost the lands on which the missions had been built. The Native Americans lost the way of life introduced by the Spanish, and they could not easily return to their

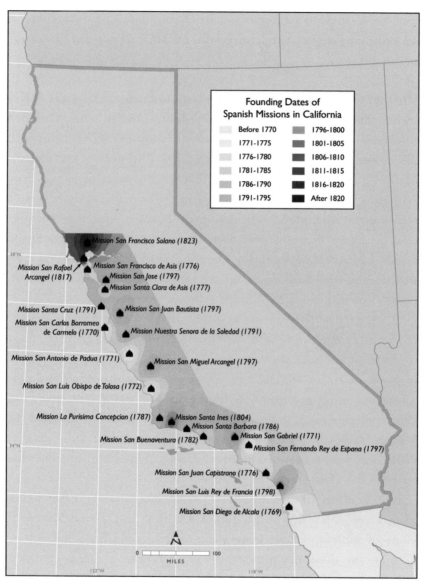

Founding Dates of
Spanish Missions in California

Before 1770	1796-1800
1771-1775	1801-1805
1776-1780	1806-1810
1781-1785	1811-1815
1786-1790	1816-1820
1791-1795	After 1820

Mission San Francisco Solano (1823)

Mission San Rafael Arcangel (1817)

Mission San Francisco de Asis (1776)
Mission San Jose (1797)
Mission Santa Clara de Asis (1777)

Mission Santa Cruz (1791)
Mission San Juan Bautista (1797)

Mission San Carlos Borromeo de Carmelo (1770)
Mission Nuestra Senora de la Soledad (1791)

Mission San Antonio de Padua (1771)
Mission San Miguel Arcangel (1797)

Mission San Luis Obispo de Tolosa (1772)

Mission La Purisima Concepcion (1787)
Mission Santa Ines (1804)
Mission Santa Barbara (1786)
Mission San Buenaventura (1782)
Mission San Gabriel (1771)
Mission San Fernando Rey de Espana (1797)

Mission San Juan Capistrano (1776)

Mission San Luis Rey de Francia (1798)

Mission San Diego de Alcala (1769)

0 [_____] 100
MILES

California Missions

traditional survival strategies. In brief, the missions' influence on Amerindians was amazingly successful in the short run but disastrous in the long run.

Missionary activity quickly followed explorations of tropical Africa and the Pacific in the eighteenth and nineteenth centuries. Competition among various Christian denominations occurred, along with the movement of Islam into the southern Philippines and eastern Africa. It was during this period that missionaries began to draw criticism. Just as earlier missionaries in California had done, newer missionaries disrupted traditional practices to the point where survival became a real concern. Some countries banned or restricted missionary activity. Nepal, for example, until recently allowed missionaries but forbade conversions to religions other than Hinduism. Its new constitution provides for religious freedom.

Missionary activity occurs regularly in US communities as well. Most visible are the Jehovah's Witnesses, who often go from door to door, sometimes with children, and the Mormons, who travel in pairs, often on bicycles and always wearing white shirts and ties. These and other groups are bringing about a significant change in church membership as the mainstream Protestant churches and the Roman Catholic Church lose members. The unification of smaller Protestant denominations and the closing of Catholic churches has changed the character of neighborhoods.

In the midst of bad publicity, some missionaries nevertheless gained accolades. Recently, Father Damien and Sister Marianne Cope of Molokai, Hawaii, were canonized by the Roman Catholic Church for their heroic service to the Hansen's disease patients at Kalaupapa. In Africa, one of the best known of all missionary-explorers was Dr. David Livingstone, who died still searching for the source of the Nile. On the other side of the continent, Albert Schweitzer, a Lutheran missionary known for his medical work, his theological writings, and his musical compositions, served in what is now the modern country of Gabon (see the map in chapter 8).

St. Damien of Molokai

NEAREST NEIGHBORS

Question 52: What major US city is closest to Honolulu?

Question 53: What European capital is closest to London?

Question 54: What two neighboring states does the Mason-Dixon Line separate?

Question 55: What neighboring countries are separated by the Palk Strait?

Question 56: Germany is separated by the Oder River from what neighboring country?

Question 57: What neighbors are separated by Offa's Dyke?

Nearest-neighbor analysis is a mathematical thingamajig that geographers have increasingly used in analyzing spatial problems. For example, if a third-world city has a large number of maternal and child health clinics to provide service to a million women, how do you assign each woman to the nearest clinic? Lacking this knowledge, some clinics may end up being deluged with patients and lack personnel or supplies to deal with the demand while others may have few patients. I actually had to deal with this problem in the Santiago, Chile, metropolitan area, and I quickly learned that "nearest" is a tricky matter. Distance that women travel to the clinic is not straight-line distance. Deviations occur for a variety of reasons, including street patterns, dangerous areas that must be avoided, and multiple-purpose trips (a woman on her way to a clinic may go to the market or visit a friend en route). Geographic information systems (GIS) have been developed that easily solve the problem I struggled with in Santiago. I worry,

however, that GIS specialists spend too much time with technical so-
lutions and not enough time prowling on foot to learn how distance
is distorted in city streets by packs of dogs, layabouts drinking wine
and harassing women who pass by, and similar barriers. Geographers
have to be knowledgeable about, and sensitive to, what's actually there;
otherwise, economists might as well create GISs.

For many geographic understandings, however, it's not necessary
to apply mathematics or even logic. Knowing where things are and
how they are located relative to other things is an important first
step in understanding how the world is put together. My students,
for the most part, had lived all their lives in Hawaii. I once asked my
introductory class of about one hundred students, "What mainland
city is closest to Honolulu?" A chorus of voices immediately said,
"Las Vegas!" Las Vegas is unquestionably the favorite destination of
many people in Hawaii. Direct scheduled flights and well-advertised
charter flights enhance the daily connectivity between Honolulu
and Las Vegas. I presume gambling is the driving force behind this
travel (although I can't be sure). Hawaii is one of the few states that
prohibits all forms of gambling; even a proposal to allow bingo was
not successful in the state legislature. It is possible that Las Vegas is
the mainland city best connected to Honolulu, but the closest large
city to Honolulu is San Francisco.

> Dr. G. says: A spokesman for the Roman Catholic bishop
> of Honolulu opposed the bingo measure with such in-
> tensity that I was astonished. In the community in which
> I grew up it was said that one could hear Catholics loudly
> praying on Friday nights, "Under the B."

*   *   *

The way we think about the location of places is often influenced
by our understanding of historical interactions. For example, the
English spent a lot of their history fighting with the French, so we

naturally assume that France and England are reasonably close in distance . . . as indeed they are. In fact, a substantial portion of today's northern France was once English territory, and the port of Calais was an important English port. Were we to add the Channel Islands and thereby consider the British Isles rather than England alone, France and England are about as close as you can get without really touching. Paris, however, is not the national capital closest to London. Amsterdam, the capital of the Netherlands, is closer.

The Mason-Dixon Line used to attract a lot more attention than it does currently. For much of US history it was said to be the boundary between the North and the South. Geographers have attempted to determine what sort of factors define these two regions of the country, and although major changes have occurred, especially in the post–World War II years, the broad generalization that the Mason-Dixon Line separates these two parts of the country is reasonably valid. It was a line created by two surveyors in the 1760s. The two principal states that it separates are Pennsylvania and Maryland. Take extra credit for your answer if you noted that it also separates Pennsylvania from Virginia (now West Virginia) and part of Delaware from Maryland.

The Palk Strait isn't much of a strait, and it does a poor job of separating India from Sri Lanka. In the "strait" between the two countries are a series of islands and coral reefs that are called Adam's Bridge on most Western maps and Rama's Bridge in India. There is sufficient open water for small boats to pass, but anything of a substantial size must go around the whole island nation of Sri Lanka. Why not build a ship channel through the bridge? That's been considered, but a Hindu Sanskrit epic tells of the god Rama skipping over this "bridge" and rescuing his wife from Sri Lanka. To destroy the natural bridge would offend those who believe the scripture. I propose that the name "Palk" be stricken from maps (Robert Palk was a British governor of Madras) and it be renamed "Rama's Strait." It would clearly be in Rama's interest to have a real strait named after him.

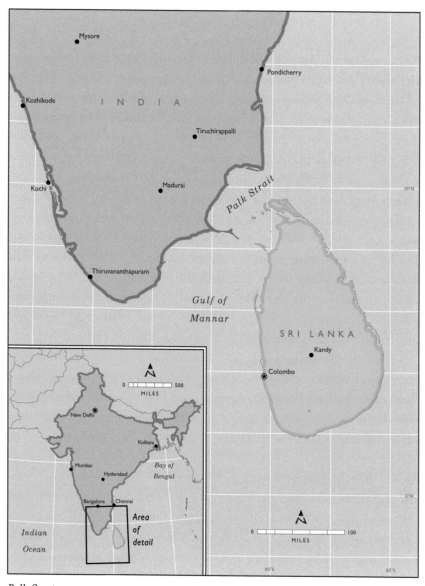

Palk Strait

*   *   *

A country called "Germany" did not exist until 1871. Until that time, Germans lived in numerous political entities in central Europe. Two of these entities were particularly powerful: Prussia and Austria. In the 1860s, Prussia waged war against Austria and, to the surprise of many, won decisively. It then declared war on France and, while the war still continued, the German states, except Austria, united into a single country. At the conclusion of the Franco-Prussian War, Germany gained control of two French provinces, Alsace and Lorraine. The Germany that emerged was the largest German state that would ever exist.

The German state is often said to be the creation of Otto von Bismarck, Germany's first chancellor. True, but ironic. In 1848, an opportunity arose to build a unified Germany from the numerous German-speaking kingdoms and duchies. Bismarck opposed unification on the grounds that it would weaken his native Prussia.

Following Germany's defeat in World War I, it not only lost territory but had its remaining territory divided by a portion of Poland that separated East Prussia from the rest of the country. After World War II, Germany lost even more territory. Its eastern boundary became the Oder River, which today separates it from Poland.

As an undergraduate, I took a course titled "The History of Britain: From Roman occupation to Queen Victoria." My notes reveal that the professor covered the period from the end of Roman occupation of Britain to Henry the VII and the Tudor dynasty—nearly a thousand years of British history—in approximately fifteen minutes. The missing thousand years, at least from a political geographic perspective, involves a progression from hundreds of minikingdoms to ever-larger territories ruled by increasingly fewer people. Boundaries between and among these holdings were disputed and often in flux unless there were clear natural boundaries (rivers, seacoasts) or man-made barriers. Hadrian's Wall, built

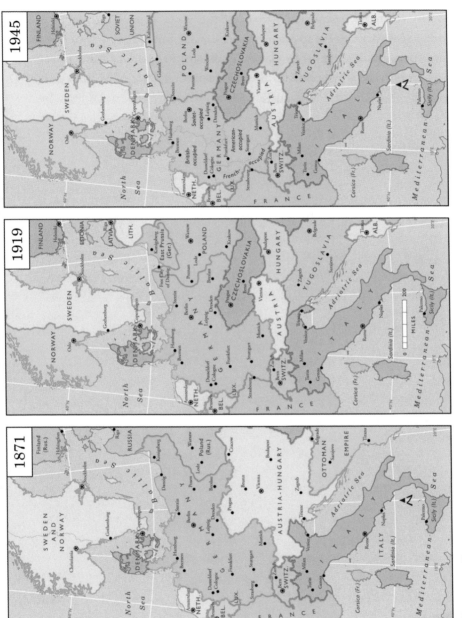

Germany, 1871–1945

by the Romans, supposedly to keep the Picts in check in what is today Scotland, was such a barrier. A similar but longer barrier was built between Wales and England. This barrier, called Offa's Dyke, still forms part of the border between modern Wales and England, now two parts of the United Kingdom.

CHAPTER 11

EXPLORERS RESCUED
FROM OBLIVION

Question 58: Who was the first to navigate through the fabled Northwest Passage?

Question 59: Who led an expedition to cross Antarctica and sailed on the Endurance*?*

Question 60: What was the American "Ex Ex" and who led it?

Question 61: What Danish explorer crossed Siberia, scaled the mountains of Kamchatka, built a ship, and explored Alaska?

Explorers were honored for hundreds of years, but the tide has changed. James Cook and Christopher Columbus are seen by some as archenemies, people who brought unwanted change, disease, domination, and exploitation of native peoples. The discipline of geography has played a significant role in this exploration denouement. The Age of Exploration, however, ought to be looked at in a different way in the twenty-first century. From what we know of mankind's origin and dispersal throughout the world, *Homo sapiens* started in only one place (Africa) and, despite minor physical differences in appearance, we still have so much in common that we all belong to the same species. We moved to survive, and along the way we adapted to an incredible range of environmental conditions (which very few other species can match). As we dispersed, we developed new languages and belief systems.

What we have witnessed in the Age of Exploration and subsequently is the reunification of the species. The number of languages has decreased, and highly localized religious beliefs have coalesced into a relatively few major religions. This process of reunification has not always gone well and sometimes has even gone backward, but for the past five hundred years or so it has been one of the most important global processes. It has occurred for the same reason that dispersal originally occurred: survival. The accumulation of resources for manufacturing, rural to urban movement, international trade, and global migration patterns can all be placed under the umbrella of species reunification. That this process has occurred, albeit slowly and with missteps, is one means by which we can measure the progress of mankind.

It is hard to blame many polar explorers for exploiting anyone. Their routes often meant they had little or no contact with native peoples. Roald Amundsen may have been the greatest of the polar explorers. He was the leader of the first expedition to successfully reach the South Pole, in 1911. It is possible that he also led the first expedition to reach the North Pole; there are some doubts about earlier claims. As if these accomplishments were not enough, Amundsen became the first person to take a ship through the Northwest Passage, the route between the Atlantic and Pacific across the northern edge of North America. Explorers had been seeking this route for hundreds of years. It took him three years, including three winters, to accomplish the journey.

Amundsen's expeditions were all characterized by careful planning and an immense knowledge of survival in polar conditions. His trip through the Northwest Passage was made on a ship only forty-five feet long and with a crew of only five. He believed that earlier attempts had been defeated by excess baggage. The particular route he took could not have been sailed by a larger ship. At one point the depth of water under his keel was only about three feet! Amundsen would probably be much more famous if he hadn't made things seem so easy.

*   *   *

It's quite possible that you never heard of Ernest Shackleton, another polar explorer. If that's so, that's not because he made things
seem easy, it's because his Antarctic adventure, initially aboard the
Endurance, was so fantastic that had it been fiction, no one would have
believed it. Indeed, Shackleton accomplished impossible things; I
count at least four.

Once Amundsen had reached the South Pole, the last task to be
accomplished by polar explorers was to cross the Antarctic continent.
This was Shackleton's plan in 1914. Before he could leave Britain,
however, World War I broke out, and Shackleton believed it would
be unpatriotic to leave on a voyage of exploration at that time. First
Lord of the Admiralty Winston Churchill, however, ordered Shackleton to go. Shackleton reached the Weddell Sea in January 1915 and
came quite close to the Antarctic continent. Pack ice impeded his
progress, and eventually his ship, the *Endurance*, became frozen in the
ice. The ship was built to withstand the ice, and the hope was that it
would be freed from the ice in the following spring.

Pressure built on the hull of the *Endurance* as the ice shifted. Eventually the ship sank, and Shackleton's crew took to the ice, moving
from floe to floe as the ice pack slowly moved to the northwest. They
took three large lifeboats with them. When the ice began to break up
beneath them, they took to the boats and eventually reached land at
Elephant Island, on the opposite side of the Weddell Sea from where
they started. When they reached the island, it was the first time they
had been on land in more than four hundred days.

Having accomplished miracle 1, Shackleton and his crew were
only marginally better off; Elephant Island was an uninhabited
wasteland. Shackleton refitted one of the lifeboats and set sail for
the nearest inhabited place, South Georgia Island, more than eight
hundred miles away. The seas were very high, the weather very bad,
and the boat on the verge of capsizing through much of the voyage. Their route had taken them to the uninhabited south coast

of South Georgia Island, and hurricane-force winds initially prevented their landing, but eventually they made it ashore (miracle 2). The weather ruled out taking the boat to the inhabited whaling station on the other side of the island, so they had no choice but to attempt to cross the mountainous island. Half the crew went, and half stayed on the shore. The climbing party managed to reach the whaling station while nearly freezing to death and without any sort of mountain-climbing gear (miracle 3).

Dr. G. says: The route Shackleton took across South Georgia Island was followed in 1955 by experienced mountain climbers. The leader of the climbing party said, in essence, Shackleton's climb was a miracle.

Shackleton immediately sent a boat to pick up the three crew members on the opposite side of South Georgia Island and then made three unsuccessful attempts to pick up the remainder of the crew on Elephant Island. Finally, he was able to borrow a ship from the Chilean navy and made a successful rescue. During this odyssey on the ice, Shackleton did not lose a single member of the *Endurance* crew (miracle 4).

The US Exploring Expedition was one of America's greatest accomplishments, but today few have heard of it. The expedition, originally authorized by Congress in 1824, when John Quincy Adams was president, did not receive funding until the following decade. It finally got under way in 1838 and continued for four years, until 1842. The expedition explored and mapped shoals and coral reefs in both the Atlantic and the Pacific, mapped the mouth of the Columbia River, mapped Samoa, visited several Pacific islands, climbed peaks in the Andes and Hawaii, and may have been the first to discover the Antarctic continent. The exploration near Antarctica was particularly noteworthy because the ships in the expedition did not

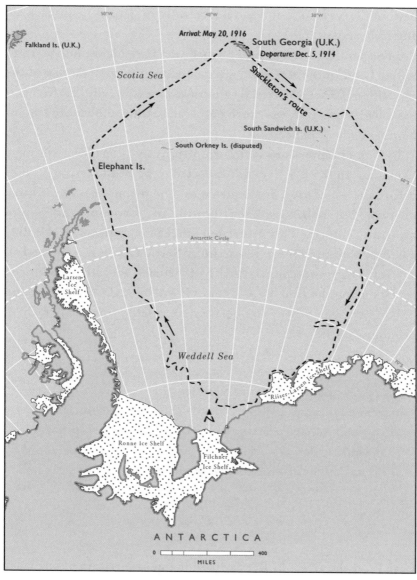

Shackleton's 1914 Expedition

have reinforced hulls and were constantly in danger from pack ice and icebergs.

The scientific findings of the expedition were highly valuable, and Wilkes Land in the Antarctic was named for the commander of the expedition, Charles Wilkes. By almost any measure, the "Ex Ex," as it was called at the time, was much more valuable than the more famous Lewis and Clark Expedition.

Its lack of fame arose from two major causes. Wilkes was only a lieutenant in the US Navy but expected to be promoted to captain before the expedition got under way. The promotion never came through, but Wilkes assumed the title of "Captain" and wore a captain's uniform. This infuriated other naval officers, and Wilkes was court-martialed for his actions. Second, Wilkes returned to a government and country that had virtually forgotten about the Ex Ex during the time he was gone. If Wilkes had only had a good public relations officer (or been one himself), things might have been much different.

Dr. G. says: It is customary in the naval services to call the commander of a ship "Captain" regardless of his rank. In this case, Wilkes commanded not only one ship but a squadron of ships. He was acquitted of this charge and several others at his court-martial.

* * *

Czar Peter the Great of Russia ruled the most territory of any ruler of any country at the time, but, like a Dr. Seuss story, he could always do with more. Peter was particularly interested in knowing whether eastern Russia was joined to the North American continent. He therefore sent a member of the Russian navy who had been born in Denmark, Vitus Bering, to find out.

You might suppose that Bering would have boarded a sailing ship in Peter's capital, St. Petersburg, and then sailed for either the Cape of Good Hope or Cape Horn. That would have been too easy. Instead, Bering began in 1725 and traveled overland across all of Russia and Siberia. Upon reaching the Pacific, Bering crossed to what we know as the Kamchatka Peninsula. Bering, however, was not sure it was a peninsula, and even if it was, he wasn't certain how far south it extended. So he crossed the high mountains of Kamchatka. Upon arriving on the other side, he built his ships and began the search of Arctic waters to determine whether Asia and North America were joined. He found the strait that was later named after him but could not sail far enough into it to determine whether the continents were

Vitus Bering's expedition being wrecked on the Aleutian Islands in 1741. Nineteenth-century illustration.

separated. He sailed back to Kamchatka, crossed to mainland Russia, and then went all the way back to St. Petersburg.

This was an incredibly long trip to gain such little information. The Russian government thought so, too, and sent him back again the same way. The second trip lasted seven years, and Bering did not make it back alive. On this trip, he discovered Kodiak Island, which was the first capital of Russian Alaska, and one of his ships discovered the mainland of Alaska.

Why were the Russians so interested in Arctic lands and waters so far from the heart of their empire? Russia's wealth had been built on the fur trade. Its movement eastward across Siberia had been largely to expand the area where it could obtain furs. Early probes into the Aleutians had uncovered seals in incredible numbers, but they had also discovered an animal whose pelt proved to be of immense value: the sea otter. Anything worth hunting, it seems, is worth hunting to extinction, and the Russians nearly did this. Only in recent years have the otters come back from the brink of extinction.

Dr. G. says: The Russians "obtained" furs rather than hunted or trapped them themselves. Native peoples in Siberia as well as Aleuts and other Alaskan natives were employed or forced to acquire the pelts.

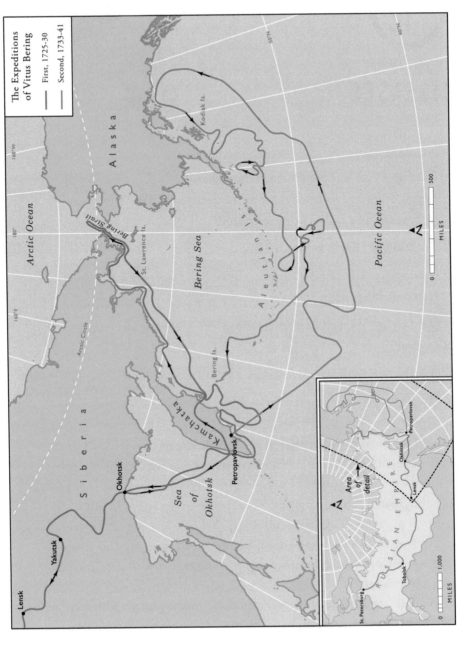

The Expeditions
of Vitus Bering

—— First, 1725-30
—— Second, 1733-41

Bering's Voyages

DISEASES

Question 62: What parasitic disease contributed to the fall of the Roman Empire, killed sixty thousand American soldiers during World War II, and continues to kill a million people each year?

Question 63: What is known as "The American Plague"?

Question 64: What disease caused a wage rise and may have led to the Protestant Reformation?

Question 65: What do we more commonly call "great pox," and where did it originate?

Question 66: What was the first disease proved to be caused by a specific bacterium?

When I began as a geographer at the University of Hawaii, one of the main specialties offered by my department was medical geography. A number of our students were simultaneously pursuing a degree in public health and an advanced degree in geography. Much of the research pursued was in epidemiology, that is, the study of the spread of disease, but there were other highly interesting studies as well. Our school of public health disappeared, and so did our medical geography faculty.

While it was around, however, medical geography provided some deliciously confrontational situations. Many people firmly believe in things that don't jibe with the evidence that medical researchers of all stripes have accumulated. Anytime a seminar touched on public water supply (with or without fluoridation), cancer "clusters," HIV/AIDS, or immunization vaccines, you could count on public "activists" showing up. Faculty were often accused of being in the pay of "big pharma," and I used to bet with a colleague about how long a discussion would go before the word "Hitler" came up as the ultimate accusation. I only regret that with the elimination of medical geography in our department I have missed all the heated discussions about GMOs!

"Bad air" killed millions over the centuries and was especially notable in the Pontine Marshes around Rome, where, in Italian, "bad air" approximates "malaria." In the days of the Roman Empire it was called simply the "Roman fever," but it was a devastating disease in China as well—and perhaps in tropical areas worldwide, although we lack evidence in these areas before European penetration. It killed sixty thousand American troops during World War II and today kills as many as one million people yearly, mostly under age fifteen.

Malaria is caused by a parasite, *Plasmodium*, and is transmitted by the female *Anopheles* mosquito. *Plasmodia* come in several varieties, but the one that causes the greatest concern is *falciparum*. Any decent, self-respecting parasite keeps its host alive in the interest of self-preservation, but *falciparum* is a poorly developed parasite that often kills its host, especially children.

Dr. G. says: After I gave a public presentation on my malaria research, I received an angry note from a faculty member in women's studies. She wrote that I should not have said that only female mosquitoes spread malaria (they are the only ones that bite people) and that "poorly developed parasite" should have been rendered as "challenged parasite." This appeared to me to be more of the politically correct nonsense wafting about campus.

Strangely, deaths due to malaria may not be as important in a given country as the morbidity associated with the disease. In Sri Lanka's dry zone and in several parts of India, malaria is hyperendemic, meaning just about everybody has the disease. With daily life interrupted by disease, even basic survival tasks are hard to accomplish. Introducing changes associated with economic development is next to impossible. Illness is a constant in affected areas.

Sri Lanka almost performed a miracle in 1946. Because malaria had been an obstacle to Allied operations in Asia and the Pacific, drugs had been developed that were better treatments than the older quinine and its derivatives. This also meant that DDT was available to Sri Lanka as "war surplus"; it is the most effective insecticide ever developed. Medicine and insecticide flowed into postwar Sri Lanka, and the death rate was cut in half in a single year. At that time, public health authorities optimistically thought that they could eradicate malaria not only from Sri Lanka but from India as well, where it was even more widespread. Sadly, this did not prove to be the case. The resurgence of malaria in South Asia and its continual presence in many tropical areas has many causes, but the immunity of mosquitoes to the pesticides and their change in behavior has been an important factor.

Dr. G. says: Mosquitoes have been observed to change their habitats when insecticides are used on a large scale.

* * *

Yellow fever was called the American plague and, indeed, it had some similarities to the black death that ravaged Europe in the fourteenth century. Cities like Memphis, New Orleans, and Birmingham—even Philadelphia, while delegates were attempting to write something nasty to send to King George III—were ravaged at intervals by yellow fever. Dr. Walter Reed, as a public health researcher in Cuba, proved that yellow fever, like malaria, was transmitted by mosquito bites, but in this case it was the female *Aedes aegypti* mosquito, not *Anopheles* mosquitoes. Strangely, sometimes mortality rates of those affected by yellow fever would run to 60 percent or higher and on other occasions to lower than 10 percent. Moreover, survivors seemed to possess immunity to the disease. This was not at all like malaria, but because malaria had been proved as both mosquito-borne and parasitic, many physicians thought yellow fever must be a parasitic disease as well.

Yellow fever is actually caused by a virus; it was the first disease ever shown to be caused by a virus. It was carried from West Africa in the blood of slaves and by mosquitoes in the holds of slave ships. Because it was a viral disease, those who recovered were totally or partially

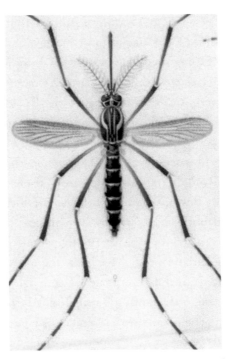

Aedes aegypti *mosquito, the vector of yellow fever*

immune to it. Today, immunization against yellow fever has greatly reduced its presence in the Western Hemisphere.

William Gorgas, a man who should be much better known and honored, applied stringent mosquito eradication programs in Cuba and virtually eliminated yellow fever from the island. Gorgas then went to Panama after the French had failed in their efforts to build a canal there. Some (myself included) believe that yellow fever and malaria were the chief obstacles to canal construction. Gorgas faced enormous resistance from officials who did not accept the "mosquito theory" but somehow managed to eradicate yellow fever from Panama as well. Since his campaign was against mosquitoes in general, the incidence of malaria was also reduced.

In the fourteenth century, Europe's population was reduced by at least one-third by the disease known as the "black death." Most of the deaths occurred in 1347. Many assumed that the disease described in accounts of the plague and its devastation was, in fact, bubonic plague. Other medical authorities disagreed, arguing that the symptoms and progression of the disease throughout Europe did not match our current understanding of the disease. The argument was only recently settled when DNA from the remains of black death victims proved that bubonic plague was the cause of death.

Medical geographic research has established that the 1347 outbreak began in Mongolia and spread along trade routes. Bubonic plague is spread by flea bites, while the fleas hitch rides on rats. The rats accompanied both land caravans and ships. Italy was especially hard hit, and recent demographic evidence shows that proportionately, Norway's population may have been the most affected.

The social and economic impacts of the plague of 1347 were enormous. On the one hand, people looked for something or someone to blame the plague on. The usual suspects were rounded up, and thousands of Jews who escaped the black death were slaughtered, along with Gypsies and lepers. Many in Europe had looked to the church to deliver them from the black death and, when it failed to do so, became disillusioned. Some scholars (myself included) speculate that this disillusionment became fertile ground for the Protestant Reformation. Finally, if we can find one good thing that came from the black death, it was that the resulting labor shortage caused wages to rise.

Great pox was first identified in Europe around 1495. The symptoms, at least in advanced cases, were somewhat similar to smallpox, but the skin lesions were larger. We know the disease better as syphilis. From a geographic perspective, the history of syphilis is especially interesting. We know syphilis existed in the New World in 1492, and we know that it didn't appear elsewhere until around 1495, when it was observed and described it Italy. There is, therefore, at least strong circumstantial evidence to suggest that Christopher Columbus's crew brought it back to Europe with them. If so, it is an amazing irony because the Spanish and other explorers exposed New World and Pacific peoples (and other isolated groups as well) to a host of contagious European diseases that caused enormous death rates and population declines. The idea (unproved) that disease could have been transmitted eastward across the Atlantic as well is another example of the power of geographic connectivity.

Europeans unquestionably carried syphilis and other diseases into Hawaii and other Pacific islands. Syphilis, however, is similar to a tropical disease endemic in some Pacific Islands, yaws. Yaws, a disease of the skin, bones, and joints, apparently confers immunity against syphilis. Several studies claim that the depopulation of Pacific islands was caused not only by higher death rates due to introduced contagious diseases but also by lower fertility due to syphilis. In those Pacific areas where yaws was endemic, population decline did not occur to the same degree that it did where there was no yaws. While the relationship between yaws, syphilis, and depopulation cannot be proved definitively (due to lack of historical data), the evidence we do have underlines that the geography and ecology of disease deserve a lot more attention than a footnote in a history text.

*   *   *

"Sanitary sewers caused polio," claimed one speaker at a conference I attended, and it's an interesting idea. The speaker's asser-
tion concerned the fact that Louis Pasteur and other scientists had
developed the germ theory of disease, the idea that these itsy-bitsy
things that can be seen only under a microscope not only make us
sick but actually kill us. The response to this idea, after the usual
resistance to any new idea had been shoved aside, was to stress
sanitation. By so "sanitizing" infants, we kept them from getting
polio at a very early age, when it usually had very little effect, and
thereby produced a population that was highly susceptible to polio
at older ages, when it is more serious or even deadly. My geographic thinking on this idea was that it was far easier to sanitize
relatively new countries, like the United States and Australia, than
it was in Europe, where infrastructure of all kinds was old or even
ancient. Certainly the idea is no stranger than the now-proved fact
that grandparents start chicken pox epidemics.

The first disease shown to be caused by bacteria is one of the oldest and most feared: leprosy, or Hansen's disease. Hansen was the
Danish scientist who proved it. While this disease has, for thousands
of years, had dreadful social and medical consequences for those
unfortunate to be infected by it, I have never been able to find any
geographic implications of the disease such as those that are associated with malaria, yellow fever, bubonic plague, or even syphilis.
So Hansen's disease is not a part of the curriculum I teach. I have,
however, been forced to bring it up in my teaching in response to
fundamentalist Christian preaching on campus.

    From time to time, Christian religious fervor seems to sweep
across my campus. In the course of my lecture on the origin and
spread of Christianity, a student asked whether it was true that the
Bible forbade homosexuality. I responded that he could look that
up for himself, but I did note that the Bible is far more full of stuff

about leprosy than anything about homosexuality. Why don't we, I asked, treat lepers according to biblical rules? This earned me a brief call from the dean.

The biblical treatment of leprosy is interesting in light of our modern understanding of the disease. Contagion seemed to be one of the main problems of concern to the Hebrews . . . and Hansen's disease is contagious. Ninety-five percent of people, however, are immune to the disease. Is it possible that the Hebrews, or possibly one of the groups they occasionally intermarried with, had a higher genetic disposition to the disease? In any case, leprosy today, although still found in the Middle East, is more likely to be found in India, Burma, or Brazil. Hawaii, both famous and infamous for its Hansen's disease colony on Molokai, still gets a fair share of new cases, but they tend to be concentrated among recent immigrants from Micronesia. Of course, we can treat the disease today. Communities like the colony on Molokai still exist because they have patients who have lived there all or most of their lives. It's their home.

POPULATION DENSITY

Question 67: What is the most densely populated country in the world?

Question 68: What is the third-largest country by population?

Question 69: What country's population is the fastest growing?

Question 70: What country is losing the most population?

Question 71: What is the largest metropolitan area in the world?

While population geography is an ancient latent subfield of geography, it came to the fore in the 1950s with an increasing public awareness of the threat posed by "overpopulation," a term that was oft used but seldom defined. The timing of the concern about population growth was ironic because explosive growth had begun way back in the early 1700s but was already beginning to taper off before the public focused its attention on it. Population geography, like the science of demography, is concerned with the tendency of population to grow (fertility), to decline (mortality), and to move from place to place (migration). By 1965, the focus of demography was almost entirely on fertility while geography remained concerned with broader issues as well as fertility.

Population density has long been a mainstay in geography textbooks (particularly older ones), although I am not sure why. Perhaps the idea is that some minimal land-to-man ratio is necessary for survival. This would hardly seem to apply, however, to the city-states and islands that have not only the highest density but are also among the richest countries (as measured by per capita income); Singapore,

Vatican City, Monaco, Bahrain, Malta, and Bermuda. In terms of countries with substantial areas, Bangladesh is far and away the most densely populated, with almost 2,500 people per square mile. One of my former students assured me that were the Australian census definition of urban places applied to Bangladesh, the entire country would be considered a city. Following Bangladesh (and ignoring city-states, islands, and small colonies), Lebanon and the Netherlands would fall second and third in the density parade. Were the entire world's population to move to California, it would not be as densely populated as the Netherlands.

At the other end of the spectrum, Mongolia is the least densely populated country, with fewer than five people per square mile. Namibia and Australia are just above Mongolia on the population density list.

Dr. G. says: Geographers have advocated a measure of density that utilizes arable (potential agricultural) land rather than all land in a country. Environmentalists, including geographers, have further modified the density concept into something called "carrying capacity," that is, the number of people who can be supported by a given amount of land. This is a useful idea if we consider the world as a whole, but attempts to apply this to smaller areas have not been impressive.

*   *   *

Three reliable and widely available sources offer population information: the United Nations, the World Bank, and the international division of the US Census Bureau, which is the source of values given in the highly popular CIA *World Factbook*. Because almost all population data are based on estimates, we often see subtle but important differences among the three sources. When it comes to population size of the world or of a country, all three sources give us roughly the same answer, with any differences due to the date when estimates or calculations were made.

The largest country in the world is China, with about 1.4 billion people, followed by India, with about 1.3 billion. An experienced census demographer who had fallen asleep twenty years ago in Bethesda or Sleepy Hollow and awoke today would be flabbergasted at these numbers. At that time, China had many more people than India, was growing about as quickly, and was expected to remain the largest country into the indefinite future. The figures now strongly suggest that India will catch and surpass China by perhaps 2025. China's growth has slowed considerably, India's only slightly. I'm sure the appearance of these two countries at the top of the list didn't surprise you; but the third-largest may. It's the United States. With nearly 320 million people, the United States is larger than Indonesia and Pakistan, the next on the list.

Population growth has two components: natural growth (or decline) and net migration. Natural growth is the excess of births over deaths and, of course, natural decline would be the excess of deaths over births. Net migration works much the same way; it is the balance of those moving in and out. Because in some countries it is difficult to estimate the number of people moving out, demographers sometimes assume migration is "negligible." In other countries, however, particularly the United States, Canada, most European countries, and countries in the Persian Gulf region, migration cannot be ignored since it can be much more important than births and deaths in affecting growth. Once births, deaths, immigration, and emigration have been determined, it's simple arithmetic to calculate growth or decline. It's customary to report growth or decline as a percentage of the total population.

When our sleeping demographer dropped off twenty years ago, it was possible to find countries with natural growth rates of 3.5 percent or higher. Now, when we see such a high growth rate, it's safe to assume that some of the growth is due to net migration. That poses a problem because net migration is always difficult to estimate. Not surprisingly, our three principal information sources have quite different answers about the fastest-growing country. The United Nations says that Liberia is the fastest-growing country, with a growth rate of about 4.6 percent annually. This seems reasonable enough; Liberia has very high fertility and is recovering from two civil wars, implying that those who fled the country may now be returning. The US Census says Libya is the fastest-growing country, with a growth rate of about 4.9 percent annually. This is also reasonable. Libya has high fertility and is also recovering from a civil war. The World Bank demurs and says Oman is the fastest-growing at a rate above 9.1 percent annually. Although Oman does have high fertility, a growth rate of this magnitude can only be accounted for by very high immigration. The labor force of Oman is mostly immigrants, largely from Indonesia, India, and the Philippines. A quick explanation: Oman has one of the world's highest per capita incomes; rich countries attract immigrants.

In the not-so-distant past, a country that lost population would do so only by catastrophe—like Ireland during the potato famine. Now, however, about thirty countries are losing population, some by natural decrease (more deaths than births), some by net out-migration, and some by a combination of both. More countries seem to be joining this list every year. Although it is a close race to the bottom, Ukraine has lost the most population, over six million, plus a still undetermined number due to the annexation of part of Ukraine, Crimea, by Russia. Ukraine's fertility is below that needed for replacement. Unless an unexpected change occurs, the number of deaths annually will soon be greater than the number of births. The movement of ethnic Russians back to Russia is the principal contributor to the decline of Ukraine's population—even before the Crimean crisis.

A close second is Russia itself. It has lost six million from its peak population but is currently growing slightly, primarily due to the immigration of ethnic Russians from other parts of the former Soviet Union. For centuries, Russia has looked to its size (distance from enemies) and its population numbers (enabling the largest standing army in Europe) as its major defenses against invasion by an enemy. With the loss of its "protective coat" of the Soviet republics *and* a decline in population, Russia has been shaken to the core. Its foreign policy needs to be viewed and evaluated in this context. Russia has embarked on a major program to recruit ethnic Russians to return to their homeland.

Dr. G. says: Russia's attempts to encourage immigration have even extended to the remnants of a nineteenth-century population of Russians who migrated to Brazil. These "Old Believers" largely remained in Brazil, but some did move to Russia. A community of Old Believers lives in Erie, Pennsylvania.

In terms of percentage decline, the Federated States of Micronesia and the Northern Marianas, both Pacific island nations, have lost the most, roughly one-fifth of their peak populations. Under current law, residents can migrate freely to the United States, and many are doing so.

City sizes in different countries are notoriously difficult to compare because "metropolitan areas" are defined differently in different countries. The idea of a metropolitan area is simple enough: a central city and a surrounding area, some of which is designated part of the central city's population, depending on the criteria used by each individual country. Using each country's own definition of a metropolitan area, the largest city by far is Tokyo, followed by Seoul and Mexico City. Obviously, we need a better and more universal definition of a metropolitan area if we wish to compare city sizes.

FLEETS

Question 72: What was the Great White Fleet?

Question 73: What was the Yellow Fleet?

Question 74: What was the Great Yellow Fleet?

Question 75: Where can you find Lakers and Salties?

Question 76: What fleet trains its officers near Ft. Baker, California, in Marin County?

We often correctly think of oceans and seas as barriers to interaction. The United States has long used both the Atlantic and the Pacific as great defensive barriers. The English have used only that tiny strip of seawater, the English Channel, as protection from its continental enemies for over a thousand years. Australia may be the best example of all since its native peoples were isolated from the rest of the world for thirty thousand years. Also, the New World was separated from the Old for twelve to fifteen thousand years. The oceans, however, are also major transportation corridors allowing greater connectivity among places. Strangely enough, the currents and winds that can carry man and his cargoes on the oceans are mentioned in the first chapter of books on physical geography but scarcely mentioned at all when we get to human geography. The scale of movement on the ocean—and the things that affect it—sometimes seem too vast for modern geography to accommodate. Even the cruise lines that have become so important to island communities escape mention in modern textbooks, despite the fact that the passengers (and tourists in general) have replaced sugarcane as the biggest revenue source (and sugar was mentioned in all the older books).

More than 70 percent of the world's population lives within 250 miles of a seacoast and millions make their livelihood on, or directly from, the oceans. It is hardly surprising that fleets of ships have been built to carry people and goods as well as to defend coasts and shipping lanes. The Phoenicians, Greeks, and Romans all relied on sea power in the Mediterranean. Later, the Vikings, while never a naval power, used the water to land their raiders on the Baltic, Atlantic, and Mediterranean coasts all the way, unbelievably, to Constantinople. We have evidence of trade across the Indian Ocean dating back to 1400 BC and some strong hints of even earlier sea connections between Southeast Asia and the Middle East.

When I think of fleets, however, I think first of the Spanish Armada and its attempt to enable an invasion of England from the Netherlands. The Spanish fleet consisted of 130 ships. They would have had an additional thirty had not the English earlier raided Cadiz and destroyed them. The English met them with about two hundred ships, albeit smaller ships and fewer guns. Or I think of arguably the most important naval battle ever fought by the United States, at Midway, when the Japanese baited and then fell into their own trap. Unlike the battle the English fought in and around the English Channel, at the Battle of Midway, the American and Japanese fleets never saw each other!

The man who truly appreciated the value of the British naval fleet and whose writings caused the United States to begin to expand its navy was Alfred Thayer Mahan. Mahan, born at West Point but a graduate of Annapolis, believed that world power was achieved not by controlling Eurasia's heartland but by controlling the rimland, the oceans. President Theodore Roosevelt was an enthusiastic supporter of Mahan's ideas, one of the reasons he was so insistent on completing the Panama Canal. In particular, Roosevelt understood the threat that Japan's navy posed for the West Coast.

In the winter of 1907, Roosevelt sent sixteen US battleships on a voyage that would last over two years and circumnavigate the globe. The intention, of course, was to wave the flag and demonstrate to the world that the United States had the capability of moving its navy to wherever its ships were needed. The ships were all painted white, the peacetime color of the U.S. Navy at that time. It became known as the Great White Fleet.

The operation was successful in several ways. Since there was no Panama Canal in 1907 (it wasn't opened until 1914), it was necessary for the fleet to pass through the Strait of Magellan, no mean feat for sixteen battleships. It was also necessary to perform maintenance on some of the ships; this required the reopening of dry-dock facilities on the West Coast. Perhaps most impressively, the fleet was supplied with adequate coal supplies despite the fact that the United States lacked coaling stations in the Pacific. This demonstration particularly impressed the Japanese, who had also become a naval power. They realized that their empire-building plans in the Pacific were going to require the neutralization of the US Navy (I wonder what they'll decide to do . . .).

In 1967, the Six-Day War broke out, with the fiercest fighting occurring between Egypt (then part of the United Arab Republic) and Israel. The Egyptians scuttled ships at both ends of the Suez Canal, thereby trapping fifteen ships that were transiting the canal. In time, most of the world forgot about them since they were trapped there for eight years. Fourteen of them were trapped in the widest part of the canal, the Great Bitter Lake. The fifteenth was between scuttled ships and in another part of the canal.

Because the desert sands swept across the canal and essentially sandblasted the trapped ships, they assumed a, well, sandy color and became known as the Yellow Fleet. Those of you with an engineering background might be interested in knowing that when the canal finally reopened, thirteen of the ships had to be towed out. The two German ships, however, emerged under their own power.

Dr. G. says: I have seen an obscure reference to another yellow fleet. Apparently the Portuguese painted their cargo and fishing boats yellow during submarine warfare in the Atlantic to indicate their neutrality. If you knew this, give yourself credit for a correct answer.

*   *   *

The fleet trapped in the Suez Canal was simply "the Yellow Fleet," but there was something else called "the Great Yellow Fleet." It is a term used to describe refrigerated railroad cars. The development of refrigeration to carry perishable crops to market was an incredibly important development in the United States because it allowed the development of market gardening in warm areas of the country and the shipment of fresh fruits and vegetables to the snowed-in north.

Famine does not happen because I didn't eat my lima beans, contrary to what my mother alleged, but because we have lacked the means to transport food from areas where it is in surplus supply to areas where it is lacking. The railroad and trucking networks in the United States provide an amazing amount of food security. Wherever there is starvation and hunger, any number of factors can be at fault; lack of food is usually not one of them.

The Great Lakes, once they were connected to the Atlantic, provided an easy transportation route from the Atlantic to the middle of North America. This is such a fundamental and incredible geographic reality that you would think public school curricula would embrace it even if geography as a whole has been assigned a place behind the "what to do when I'm arrested" unit in the social studies curriculum. Unfortunately, however, the Great Lakes remain a great unknown to many. My earliest memory of the Great Lakes was listening to the loading of a collier at Sodus Bay, New York, on Lake Ontario. The ship, as I recall, was the *Fontana*, and it was loaded by coal cars coming by railroad from Pennsylvania. Once loaded, the *Fontana* carried the coal to Oswego, New York, and off-loaded it for use by an electrical generating plant. It is impossible to describe adequately the loading process. If perhaps you can imagine your neighbor pouring marbles or pennies into a pail all night long and using a PA amplifier so that it can be heard miles away, you will at least have an inkling. The *Fontana* was not a huge ship, but the Great Lakes used to have (and to some extent still has) some good-sized vessels.

Dr. G. says: Are you an NBA fan? Do you know the Los Angeles Lakers were formerly the Minneapolis Lakers?

When the St. Lawrence Seaway opened, it permitted seagoing vessels to enter the Great Lakes. A ship that could make it through the seaway could go anyplace on the Great Lakes—but it did not work the other way around. Several of the ships that plied the Great Lakes were too big to make it through the seaway. So, at any given time, there are two basic kinds of ships on the Great Lakes: those that can navigate only on the lakes ("lakers") and those that can travel both on the lakes and the oceans ("salties").

While I hesitate to combine geography with a more prosaic science like physics, it is probably worth noting that salties can pick up a full load of widgets in Duluth, proceed through the Great Lakes to the seaway, and then add more widgets to the cargo at Montreal as they begin to encounter saltier water. Seawater provides more buoyancy than freshwater, thus the ship can take on an additional load.

*   *   *

Within sight of the Golden Gate Bridge, a service academy will be located when construction is completed in 2061. This is Starfleet Academy, alma mater (to be) of James Tiberius Kirk, Spock, and other officers of the *Enterprise*. Starfleet was perhaps not aware that the academy will virtually straddle the San Andreas Fault. While Captain Kirk is clearly modeled after Captain Cook (who said, approximately, "I desire to go where no man has gone before"), the *Star Trek* series could have benefitted from a living geographer as an advisor.

SPICE SEEKERS

Question 77: In what island group do we find Tenate, Tidore, Pulau Mauri, Makian, and Bacan?

Question 78: Black pepper is native to what country?

Question 79: What is Connecticut's nickname . . . and why?

Question 80: Cinnamon is native to what country?

Question 81: What do chili peppers, pineapple, chocolate, and vanilla have in common?

Some explorers, like Cook and Lewis and Clarke, actually explored. Most of those whom we call "explorers" were not really exploring but searching for specific things. Columbus was not looking for a New World (and never knew he'd found one) or trying to prove the world was round (most people knew that and still do, excepting certain US politicians). Yes, he was trying to find a new route to Asia, but he wanted that new route for one reason: spices. Historians have changed their stories over the years as to why spices were so prized in Europe, but what we can say for certain is that spices were incredibly valuable there. While we don't have an easy means of comparing monetary values and volume measures, the story of Ferdinand Magellan's voyage is revealing.

Magellan set sail with five ships seeking to enable Spain to find a westward route to Asia to better the route Portugal already had around Africa to India. Magellan lost four of his ships along the way, and he lost his life in the Philippines. Of the 270 men who left on the voyage, only 18 made it back—and they were on the verge of starvation in a ship that had most of its sails blown out in the homeward rounding of the Cape of Good Hope. If you had been an investor in this voyage, you would have been very disappointed to learn its fate, but unbelievably, after Magellan's death the new commander, Juan Sebastian Elcano, had found the tiny Moluccas Islands of Ternate, Tidore, Pulau Mauri, Makian, and Bacan, the only place in the world where cloves grew. The lone surviving ship, the *Victoria*, had purchased enough cloves so that the entire expedition made a profit.

Three spices, cloves, nutmeg, and mace, came from the Moluccas and nowhere else on earth in the fifteenth and early sixteenth centuries. These are the prizes Columbus was after . . . and he thought he'd found them. At first his story to Ferdinand and Isabella was that he'd found the Indies where the spices grew but had arrived at the wrong time of year, before the cloves and nutmeg were ripe. He did bring "cinnamon" back with him, but it had somehow spoiled during the voyage (whatever he actually had was not cinnamon). On later voyages, spices seemed just out of his reach; if only he could sail a little farther west, he assured royalty and others in Spain, the Spice Islands were right there. Actually, they were about eight thousand miles out of his reach.

Dr. G. says: Nutmeg and mace come from the same tree.

* * *

The Portuguese, the most westward located of Europeans, began the search for spices by making increasingly long voyages along the west coast of Africa. Bartholomew Diaz eventually reached the southern tip of Africa and later was to play a major role in the Portuguese takeover of the spice trade. Portuguese spice hunter Vasco da Gama finally reached India before Columbus ever set sail. There the Portuguese found the spices they were looking for, but

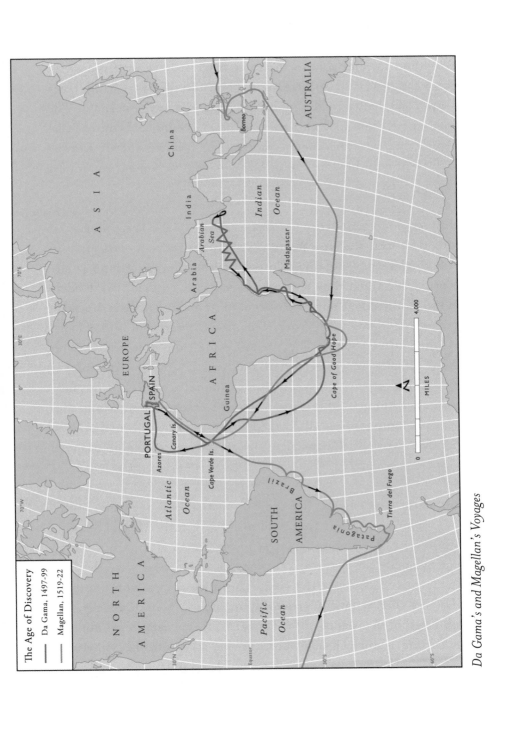

The Age of Discovery
— Da Gama, 1497-99
— Magellan, 1519-22

Da Gama's and Magellan's Voyages

cloves and nutmeg sold in the spice markets were far from where they were grown and so were no bargain. On the other hand, black pepper was native to the Malabar Coast in southwest India. The Portuguese came to dominate (but never completely control) the pepper trade. In turn, pepper became the favorite spice in Europe and eventually became cheap enough so that even commoners could afford at least a small supply.

Nutmeg, also native to a few small islands in the East Indies, was sought all over the New World. Even the Pilgrims looked for it in New England. Eventually, colonial America began to import nutmeg; even by that time it was still a valuable commodity. Traders in the Connecticut ports were accused of making wooden nutmegs and selling them in New York. This gave Connecticut its nickname of "the Nutmeg State." There is some question, however, whether there actually were counterfeit nutmegs on the market coming from Connecticut. Apparently some, unfamiliar with how nutmegs were used, thought of them as nuts to be cracked open. When they tried, of course, they discovered the nutmeg was "wooden." So rightly or wrongly, Connecticut traders got the reputation of being slippery operators.

In a sense, cinnamon is like the Connecticut nutmeg story, but in the case of cinnamon, almost all of it used in the United States is counterfeit. Cinnamon is native to Sri Lanka (formerly Ceylon) and probably the main reason that the Portuguese were the first Europeans to colonize the area. The spice comes from the bark of a tree that originally grew only in the wet zone (basically, the southwest of the island) of Sri Lanka. While cinnamon was popular in Europe, a much cheaper substitute was also available. Sometimes called "Chinese cinnamon," cassia is related to true cinnamon but lacks the pungent, deep taste of the real stuff. Almost all "cinnamon" sold in the United States is cassia. In Europe, both in the days when spice was king and today, a distinction is made between cinnamon and cassia.

Controlling the source of spices, an area from India's Malabar Coast to the islands of Indonesia, was a contest between the seafaring powers of Europe from approximately 1490 until 1767. Portugal got there first, but there was the matter of the Treaty of Tordesillas. In this treaty, Spain and Portugal divided the world between them. The dividing line, established in 1494, was measured from the Cape Verde Islands, but the difficulty was that no one was able to measure longitude accurately enough at the time to tell where the line actually was. Portugal got everything east of the line; Spain got everything to the west. Because the line only divided the Western Hemisphere, the right to colonize the Eastern Hemisphere was still up for grabs. Subsequent treaties attempted to correct this, but remember, the only real issue was who could control the Moluccas and their spices. If we use modern navigational systems, we know that regardless of what treaty was invoked, Portugal had rights to the Spice Islands. This despite the fact that Magellan, Portuguese himself but sailing for Spain (or at least his surviving crew), got there first. This was a true diplomatic mess.

Dr. G. says: When Argentina invaded the Falkland Islands in 1982, they cited the Treaty of Tordesillas as justification.

By the seventeenth century, the disagreement between Spain and Portugal over the Spice Islands was rendered moot by the fact that the Dutch East Indies Company had taken over all of modern Indonesia and gained Sri Lanka as well. The Dutch held the spice trade under much tighter control than the Portuguese had ever been able to accomplish, but smuggling was still rampant, particularly by the British.

* * *

Ironically, while Europeans went everywhere in the New World looking for spices that weren't there, they overlooked flavors native to the
Americas that would outdo the spices and plants of Asia. Although
Columbus took cacao back with him from his fourth voyage in 1502,
it was nearly two hundred years before chocolate became well established in Europe. Vanilla, a native of Mexico, was little known in
Europe until the nineteenth century. It is derived from an orchid,
but the orchid could be pollinated only by a bee native to Mexico.
Readers of my earlier book will know that I highly recommend a visit
to the Hawaiian Vanilla Company on the island of Hawaii. There
visitors will learn about the history, cultivation, and use of vanilla
from Jim and Ian Reddekopp. Wise visitors will sample the cuisine
that Chef Tracy Reddekopp has developed using vanilla as a spice to
blend with and enhance the flavor of other foods. Consider today
how much chocolate and vanilla are used in the world compared to
the cloves and nutmeg the Spanish were seeking.

The New World also was the home of the chili pepper, a spice that
has been adopted by Koreans, Burmese, Thais, and Basques plus
other groups who today have little idea that it originated in Central America. Finally, the pineapple, hardly a spice, but a fruit and
flavor, is native to South America but perfected by its cultivation in
Hawaii. Chocolate, vanilla, pineapple, and the chili pepper, all native to the Americas and all put on the back shelf by the spice seekers.

PRINCIPAL (RARE) PRODUCTS

Question 82: How did fuller's earth get its name, and in what entertainment industry is it used extensively?

Question 83: In what country was yttrium discovered?

Question 84: In Australia, suri and huacaya are used to protect lambs from fox attacks. Where did these protective animals originate?

Question 85: What is the most valuable spice today (per unit of weight)?

Question 86: Who, during an expedition to the high Andes, discovered chickens that laid square eggs?

Woe to those introduced to geography through principal products. When I first began teaching introductory geography to university students, I replaced an instructor who gave me copies of the exams he used. I discovered that about 80 percent of his questions dealt with the countries producing the most of this or with the greatest reserves of that . . . in other words, principal products. Actually, this type of question may have made up more than 80 percent of the exam questions; I fell asleep before I could finish reading them.

There are two things wrong with the "principal products" approach (not counting its sleep-inducing effect). Scientists have developed organizing principles called theories that enable us to put our facts in a row. Theories are a matter of convenience. If new facts come along that don't fit in a theory, we throw out the theory, not the facts. Complex sciences like chemistry or geography would become so bogged down in factual detail that they would grind to a halt without theories. In the same way, classroom lectures or textbooks need to have organizing principles. This certainly does not mean that natural resources or mineral reserves or other kinds of "principal products" are not important; rather, they need to be put in a context or framework where we can understand *why* they are important.

The second thing wrong with the memorization of endless facts is that facts keep changing. My predecessor's exams now have different answers. Sudbury, Ontario, for example, once the "Nickel Capital of the World," still produces nickel, but now not as much as the Philippines. Bauxite, which the exam answers said comes from Jamaica and Suriname, now comes from Australia. Someone who took this course forty years ago would be in for a few shocks today.

Many think a country's wealth is measured by its inventory of natural resources. In the short run, we can look at countries like Kuwait and Qatar and see how petroleum resources have enriched them, but we can't account for Switzerland and Japan this way. They're among the most prosperous countries, but they lack natural resources.

Some of my students, especially from Pacific island nations, had trouble with basic ideas associated with natural resources. Things that most American students take for granted, like a coal mine or "drilling for oil" or a hydroelectric power dam, are simply unfamiliar concepts to those who live where there are no mines, no drilling, and no rivers. Once, after I had delivered a lecture on coking ovens in western Pennsylvania and their role in the steel industry (and their pollution), one student asked, "They must have used it in, like, great big tanker trucks, not out of little green bottles, right?" This student, however, was not from Micronesia but from California.

I think I made a huge mistake in not including fuller's earth in my teaching—it just seems so darned appropriate. A "fuller" handles

Dr. G. says: Coke is to coal as charcoal is to wood.

sheepskins and is mainly a felt maker. Wool, however, is greasy, but my ancestors discovered that a type of clay, originally found in Britain, had the ability to absorb oils and grease. It could be rubbed into the wool and then brushed or washed out, thus removing the grease.

Today the United States is by far the biggest producer of fuller's earth—and by far the biggest consumer. The motion picture industry is one of the biggest users, where fuller's earth fills a variety of needs. Explosions seen in movies often use fuller's earth since it creates more bang for the buck; a blast seems much bigger when fuller's earth is what is actually being blown up. It is also used in makeup, to artificially "age" sets or clothing, and to convert a paved road into a seemingly unpaved one.

Fuller's earth is not a rare earth, and, strangely, rare earths are not rare. Rare earths include twenty-five elements, all but one of which are reasonably abundant in the earth's crust. The single truly rare earth, promethium, is radioactive. These elements are called "rare" because the minerals in which the elements are found are low grade, that is, the concentration of the elements in the minerals is so low that it is very expensive to mine and extract the elements.

Yttrium, one of the rare earths, contains the element terbium (Tb, atomic number 65) which is used in green phosphors for color television and fluorescent lights. It also contains yttrium (Y, atomic number 39), which has many uses, including the production of red phosphors on your TV screen. Yttrium, the mineral, also contains at least two other rare earth elements. By now, I'm sure you've figured out that yttrium was named after the village of Ytterby in Sweden, where rare earths were first identified and extracted.

Today, China is the largest producer of rare earths and has become a bit greedy by restricting the amount that can be exported. This, of course, has the effect of driving up the price and has stimulated penny-stock peddlers and others to promote rare earths as great investment opportunities. The word "rare" is the best selling point. My advice is to remember that rare earths are not rare, and as the price goes up, it will stimulate extraction elsewhere.

Suri and huacaya are among my favorite animals. They are types of alpacas, those animals that look like small llamas and produce very high-quality wool. They are native to South America and often are given names like Carlos and Juan. While they are raised in the United States, my limited research reveals that there has been no effective marketing system developed for their wool. The Australians, however, seem to have developed such a system. Moreover, they have discovered that a mix of alpacas and sheep has produced an interesting phenomenon. Some sheep-raising areas are heavily infested with foxes that feast on the lambs. Alpacas are protective of the lambs, and anecdotal evidence shows that more lambs survive when the alpacas are around.

Dr. G. says: Huacaya have a coat that looks like a sheep's fleece, while Suri have a fur that appears knotted or kinky. Here's a bonus piece of trivia: baby alpacas are called "cria."

Alpaca

* * *

In a previous chapter, I wrote about the search for spices. At the time of the Great Spice Hunt, it is highly likely that cloves and nutmegs were the most valuable by unit of weight, followed by cinnamon and black pepper. Things have changed today, and the most valuable spice is one that was, and is, grown in Europe: saffron.

Saffron may have originated in Crete. It comes from the "threads" or stigma of the saffron crocus. It was first cultivated in Greece and later spread to Italy, France, Spain, and England. It was introduced to the Amish area of Pennsylvania and is still grown today in Lancaster County. Although culinary experts argue about the best saffron, some claim that the saffron called "mancha" from Spain is the best.

Perhaps you've heard that the SAT, the classic admissions test for college, has been changed. I will not say "watered down" (although others have). A late-night TV show alleged that a new SAT question was, "What is the principal ingredient in meatloaf?" I have often argued that exams of this sort should test not only knowledge and reasoning ability but also creativity, persistence, and poise under pressure. With this in mind, for years in MA oral exams, I used a photograph of a saffron crocus field in Spain that featured an old wooden windmill in the background. I'd ask the candidate where the photograph was taken. Only about 10 percent ever got it right, but when one did, the eyes of the candidate would light up and the answer would tumble out. One or two identified not only Spain but La Mancha (from Don Quixote's evil windmills). I noted over the years that those who answered the question not only finished their degree pursuit more quickly than others but seemed (as nearly as I could gauge) to be much more successful professionally.

Dr. G. says: Don Quixote was from the town of La Mancha, where the crocus grows!

* * *

Walt Disney's Comics and Stories, led by artists Carl Barks and Don Rosa, introduced children to the geography of many parts of the world. Everywhere from Easter Island through aboriginal customs and beliefs in Australia to Teddy Roosevelt in the Badlands of South Dakota were described and drawn with wonderful detail and delightful plots. Often, Duck expeditions were financed by superrich Scrooge McDuck, who usually brought along his relatives Donald, Huey, Dewey, and Louie. For many children in the 1950s and 1960s, the greatest of these stories was the adventure of Donald and his three nephews in the Andes of Peru, where, among other things, they found chickens that laid square eggs.

PIRATES

Question 87: *Where did the Barbary Corsairs ply their trade?*

Question 88: *Who was the most successful pirate in the Caribbean?*

Question 89: *What pirate left the business to become lieutenant governor of Jamaica?*

Question 90: *What pirate aided the United States at the Battle of New Orleans?*

Question 91: *What famous Pirate was born in Carolina, Puerto Rico, and died off the coast of San Juan?*

Piracy can be dated to the fourteenth century BC and probably existed from the time when people first put valuable things in boats. Good pirates had to be good geographers, both to navigate and to identify places where they could find proper prey. In the Golden Age of Piracy (c. 1650–1730) and for centuries earlier, sailing ships were both the hunted and the hunters. The winds and currents dictated where ships could go. Once departing ports and approximate destinations were known, calculating routes was relatively easy. In turn, pirates could build their bases so as to intercept ships taking those routes.

In the Mediterranean, piracy did not necessarily require the geographic skills needed elsewhere; it is somewhat like boats in a bathtub. The Roman Empire was plagued by pirates for centuries. At times, this provoked fierce conflict, while at other times the empire reached a truce or even full cooperation with the pirates. By the

Middle Ages, piracy became embedded in areas along the northern shore of Africa. Although the pirates, who specialized in the Western Mediterranean, were mostly Islamic, other groups, known collectively as the Barbary Corsairs, also operated. In addition to the normal pirate booty, the Barbary Corsairs engaged in kidnapping, sometimes holding victims for ransom and sometimes selling them into slavery. This was a huge operation. One estimate is that the Barbary Corsairs sold more than one million Europeans into slavery either in North Africa or in the Ottoman Empire.

The United States had trouble with the Barbary Corsairs early in its history. The pirates there, despite treaties with the United States, demanded that tribute be paid for free passage. The political rhetoric in the United States was "Millions for defense; not one cent for tribute," but the reality was that 20 percent of the US budget was spent on tribute payments. The Barbary Corsairs were the biggest reason for the establishment of the US Navy. The "Marine Corps Hymn" reference to the "shores of Tripoli" attests to the fact that problems between the United States and Islamic peoples are not of recent vintage.

Dr. G. says: Morocco was the first nation to recognize US independence. It also appears to have been the first to break a treaty with the United States since it demanded that tribute be paid for free passage in its territorial waters.

* * *

The beginnings of piracy in the Caribbean can be traced to the farm animals the Spanish had put ashore to enable the survival of shipwrecked sailors. In fact, sailors were shipwrecked and did survive on these animals. The sailors were also able to lure ships ashore for the meat they could provide. From there, it was a fairly easy step to

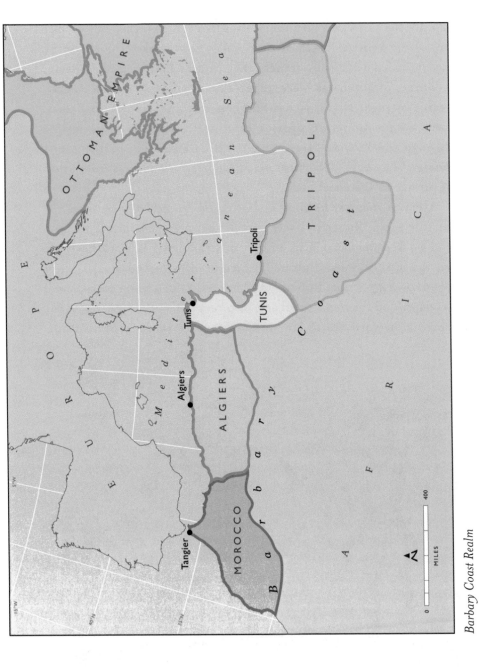

Barbary Coast Realm

capture the ships and turn themselves from shipwrecked sailors into full-fledged pirates. Because these early crews cooked their meat on a grill, called a *boucon* in French, they became known as buccaneers.

Three pirate bases were especially important in the Caribbean: Tortuga Island, Kingston, Jamaica, and Nassau, Bahamas. Each was positioned to provide easy interception of ships passing through the Florida Strait, the Windward Passage, or the Mona Passage. The base at Tortuga may have been the largest infestation of pirates in the Caribbean.

A movie that has become a classic (*The Princess Bride*) features the terrible pirate Roberts. There actually was a terrible pirate Roberts who worked the Caribbean and was better known as Black Bart. He was the most successful pirate, as measured by the number of ships taken: over 470. Bart Roberts (and others) raided shore areas as well as committed the more usual acts of piracy at sea. Bart was noted for hanging the governor of Martinique from the yardarm of his ship.

Pirate Black Bart Roberts

* * *

Apparently, *Forbes* magazine published a list of the richest pirates, and number nine on the list was Henry Morgan. Like Bart Roberts, Morgan was born in Wales. His career became legendary when he decided to skip the middleman and attack depositories of Spanish gold *before* they set sail. He attacked the city of Cartagena, which was surrounded by high walls and protected by large cannons. He was unsuccessful, but he later attacked Panama City and this time won the day, carrying off huge supplies of Spanish gold, which he took back to England. Morgan, however, was brought to trial because England had a peace treaty with Spain that protected Panama. Morgan was able to prove that he knew nothing of the treaty. Relations between England and Spain were already deteriorating at the time, and Morgan ended up being knighted for the same act for which he had been tried in court. He later became lieutenant governor of Jamaica and left an estate of over $14 million.

Why were pirates like Roberts and Morgan so successful? The largest source of seamen in the world from at least the seventeenth century to the nineteenth was England. Its merchant fleets and the Royal Navy required enormous manpower, and working conditions for the sailors were only a small step above slavery. Even ships' officers existed on minimal and uncertain pay. From time to time, Britain would reduce its naval forces and thereby put ashore thousands of seamen. Comparisons of pay show that pirates did considerably better than sailors in the Royal Navy or the merchant fleet. Pirates

Dr. G. says: Naval ships separated officers from common seamen by a system of strict discipline. Pirate ships maintained the same separation because their officers were the only ones who knew how to navigate. The average pirate knew everything about a sailing ship except how to navigate it.

lived a more democratic and easier life . . . unless they were caught. Even the noose could be avoided by privateering, that is, piracy authorized by one country against other countries.

One of the most famous privateers was the French pirate Jean Lafitte. He was a leftover from the Golden Age of Piracy and had managed to stay in business by preying on ships near the Louisiana and Texas coasts. Surprisingly little is known about Lafitte; even the spelling of his name is in doubt. He apparently was of considerable help to the American forces at the Battle of New Orleans in 1814, both by providing intelligence to the Americans and by interfering with British supplies to their troops.

One of the most famous Pirates of all time was born in Carolina, Puerto Rico, and died in a plane crash after taking off from San Juan, Puerto Rico: Roberto Clemente. Clemente began his baseball career as a benchwarmer for a Puerto Rican team and then was drafted by the Dodgers, who sent him to Montreal, where again he mostly rode the bench. After being drafted in the rookie draft by the Pittsburgh Pirates, he began a seventeen-year career that made him one of the best baseball players ever. Clemente was among the first Caribbean players in the majors and one of the first of African descent as well. He always struck me as a stranger in a strange land, never comfortable among non-Spanish players or in the climate of Pittsburgh. As a player, he was incredible. Early in his career, he was known to possess great fielding and throwing prowess but was a weak batter. He finished his career with a .317 lifetime average and got his three thousandth hit in his last game. He was killed on a humanitarian mission to Central America. Baseball waived the normal five-year waiting period and elected Clemente immediately to the Baseball Hall of Fame. Clemente was really the first Pirate of the Caribbean!

Piracy continues in modern times and is probably more lucrative now than ever. The technique has changed, with modern pirates using small, very fast craft and automatic weapons. Their aim is not to steal the cargo of a ship but to hold the crew, the ship, and its cargo hostage. According to some estimates, this form of piracy is a billion-dollar business. The epicenter is the coast of Somalia, but West Africa and the Moluccas Islands are also danger areas. While international cooperation has reduced modern piracy to some extent, the secret to the success of piracy is to have a base in a country that is either unable or unwilling to disturb the shore base. Find a country whose government does not really control its own territory and you, too, can have your own piracy operation.

IMAGINARY/MYTHICAL/ LEGENDARY PLACES

Question 92: Where was El Dorado?

Question 93: What was Cockaigne?

Question 94: On what plot of land do Wol and Woozles live?

Question 95: What was Cibola?

Question 96: Where was Brigadoon?

Question 97: Where was Shangri La?

In a math class in high school, I was introduced to an imaginary number, the square root of negative one. As I thought about this, the idea became exciting: Do imaginary numbers obey the same rules as regular numbers? Can I add them, or can I imagine how they might be added? If two people worked a problem using imaginary numbers, would they necessarily get the same answer? This concept proved frustrating because through additional years of high school math and four semesters more in college, imaginary numbers were never mentioned again. Had I only imagined them in the first place?

Imaginary places in geography may be more important than imaginary numbers. A great many expeditions were begun to find places that never existed. Along the way, real things and places were found that were of immense value, but they were ignored at the time. Young children, I think, may benefit from reading about imaginary places. Aside from learning rudimentary geography, children can find a sanctuary in places like Pooh's house or Peter Rabbit's burrow.

The Spanish, in their quest to find riches in the Americas, eventually succeeded, but they endured a great deal of frustration along the way for two reasons: they didn't understand the value of what they did find, and they chased after mythical places. Several of the plants they found (especially maize and potatoes) would eventually revolutionize European agriculture, but it would take two hundred years or so before this happened. Meanwhile, explorers combed the rain forest and mountains of South America looking for fabled cities of gold.

El Dorado was the object of two centuries of searching. El Dorado, "the golden one," apparently referred to a man. The one who was to become chief of the Muisca tribe in Colombia was covered in gold dust and then washed it off in Lake Guatavita. At the same time, gold objects were also thrown into the lake. The Spanish attempted to drain the lake several times and, in fact, a few gold items were recovered. So if you answered "Colombia" to this, give yourself credit for a correct answer.

The legend of El Dorado grew over the years to the point where it was forgotten that the term referred to a man. It first became a golden city and then a golden kingdom. The Spanish searched everywhere in the Andes and in the Upper Amazon basin for it. Francisco Orellana, during such a search, was the first to travel down the length of the Amazon.

Dr. G. says: Orellana's description of the Amazon shoreline included endless villages, even cities—in other words, a heavily populated region. Other earlier explorers made similar observations. A century or so later, there was no such population concentration. Were Orellana and others exaggerating? Possibly, but here's a case where archeology won't help much. The rain forest would quickly obliterate any signs of settlement.

El Dorado became so embedded in Spanish thinking that it actually appeared on maps that were not discredited until the nineteenth century. Since there actually was no El Dorado—the city or the kingdom—we obviously can't pinpoint a location. On at least one old map, however, it is shown as being in present-day Guyana. If you so answered, count it correct.

Cockaigne was a medieval peasant's utopia. It offered everything that was in short supply for the average person in the Middle Ages: food, leisure, alcohol, spices, sex, and general debauchery. Over time, the term came to be used for both Paris and London. The fantasy of an ideal place stimulated a great deal of geographic exploration, perhaps more than we think today. El Dorado was a place like Cockaigne, certainly equally fantastic. Searching for the source of the Nile and for the ultimate source for spices somewhere to the east is part of the same mystique.

Dr. G. says: "Utopia" is a word contrived from the Greek by Thomas More. Literally, it means "nowhere."

When Captain Cook arrived in both Tahiti and Hawaii, tales of Cockaigne must have been in the minds of the crew. Here were places that offered a reality that seemed utopian. Even today, travelers to these and other distant places expect the unusual and hope for the ideal; tourism seems driven by the same forces that drove exploration in an earlier age.

A. A. Milne bought a house near Ashdown Forest, an easy drive from London. Within three years of his move, he had written extensively about inhabitants of the forest, which for his writings shrank from five hundred acres to "100 akers." The bear that was the central character lived under the name of Mr. Sanders, which might have implied he was an undercover operative except that there seemed little to spy on. The character in *Winnie-the-Pooh* that I can most relate to is Owl because he seemed to me to be stereotypical of university administrators, who, given half a chance, can be incredibly articulate without saying much at all. Owl's most obvious shortcoming was his inability to read and write, which is why he is known as "Wol" to the literati. Woozles never actually appeared in person in Milne's writings, but they were fearful creatures that lived in the North.

Pooh has been analyzed and dissected from so many angles that it is hard to believe he was merely a stuffed toy. Yes, a geography has been written about the 100 Aker Wood, and *Winnie Ille Pooh* is the only book written in Latin to appear on the *New York Times* best-seller list. E. H. Shepherd's illustrations and his cartography have become legendary. Disney's interpretation of Pooh and friends has been one of the studio's most profitable undertakings but, if you'll indulge my modest opinion, was also one of the great abominations in the long history of movie-making imitations of great literature.

Cibola is the North American equivalent of El Dorado. Its existence was reported by Spanish survivors of a shipwreck; from their captors they learned of seven cities of gold called Cibola. The Spanish explorer Francisco Coronado trekked across Kansas and Nebraska looking for the cities but found only native dwellings. Other, smaller expeditions were also launched, and from time to time rumors about the location of Cibola emerge. If you'd like the exact location, a county in New Mexico and a town in Arizona are named Cibola.

Many who saw either the musical *Brigadoon* on Broadway or the movie thought it was about a legendary Scottish town. In fact, composers Lerner and Loewe denied that it had come from anything other than their imaginations. Apparently, however, there are several stories of legendary towns that disappear and then reappear. In any case, Brigadoon is supposed to be in Scotland.

As a geographer, one of the things that I found fascinating about *Brigadoon*, which first appeared in 1947, was that it presaged the depopulation of rural areas in the United States (that is, those outside risk of capture by expanding suburbs). While I personally know of several rural villages that have either totally disappeared or are on the verge of abandonment, I am not personally acquainted with any geographic study that addresses this issue. Look to chapter 20 for a discussion of depopulation.

About six years after Milne introduced us to the 100 Aker Wood and a decade before *Brigadoon* appeared, British author James Hilton's novel *Lost Horizon* attracted worldwide attention. In the novel, a utopian valley, Shangri La, appeared, and the name eventually became a common expression in the English language referring to an ideal place or earthly paradise. Much like the Spanish explorers centuries earlier who tried to find El Dorado and Cibola, people all over the world tried to determine where Shangri La was—just as if it were a real place. *National Geographic* magazine was scanned for articles that dealt with Buddhist areas in the Himalayas for clues. The Nazis actually sent an agent to the Himalayas to find Shangri La, apparently because its existence would lend credence to their "Aryan" theory of a super race. Possible locations ranged from the Hunza Valley in northern Pakistan to Yunnan Province, China. Take your pick. It was a fictional place!

DEEP IN THE
HEART OF . . .

Question 98: What do Lebanon, Kansas, Belle Fourche, South Dakota, and Plato, Missouri, have in common?

Question 99: The Mapocho River flows through the center of what city?

Question 100: "One if by land, two if by sea, and I on the opposite shore will be." The opposite shore of what river?

Question 101: What Spanish territory was originally known as the New Philippines?

Question 102: Where is the Zocalo (the original only, no copycats allowed)?

Question 103: How do the inner and outer core of the earth differ?

Central Place Theory, one of geography's important contributions to an understanding of aspects of human behavior, has always impressed me because it explains something we all can observe but hardly ever notice: cities and towns are not all the same size. In my days of trying to become a geographer at Penn State, a visiting professor went on an absolute tirade about this theory, arguing that it was racist. Later, a colleague of mine insisted Central Place Theory was of no value because it was "Eurocentric." Later still, a student in one of my classes objected that it was "sexist." I suppose there is some truth in all these objections. If, for example, we consider nomadic people, then we have no urban places to consider (although certain aspects of the theory, since it explains how people arrange themselves in space, would apply to aspects of even nomadic life).

There are aspects of centrality, however, to which none of these objections apply. The composition and density of the earth's center obviously is not influenced by race or gender bias on the part of us living on the crust. Iconic landmarks, similarly, identify places to us in much the same way that an average summarizes a list of numbers. The Thames is a central feature of London, the Empire State Building tells us we are in New York, and the Eiffel Tower, that we are in Paris.

Be honest now—if you tried to answer question 98 above, you were tempted to say, "What they have in common is that I've never been to any of those places and I don't intend to go." Don't be rash. There might be good reason to visit these places if you're a geographer at heart. A few miles from Lebanon, Kansas, (the precise location is a difficult calculation) is the geographical center of the contiguous United States. Near Belle Fourche, South Dakota, is the geographical center of all fifty states. When Alaska was added to the Union in 1959, the largest state by far, the geographic center of the country moved far to the north; Hawaii's admission in the same year had a much smaller influence because of its much smaller size. Plato, Missouri, is the population center of the United States based on the census of 2010. This is perhaps the most interesting central point because it is constantly changing. In the first census of 1790, the population center was in Maryland, about fifty miles from Washington, DC. Since then it has moved steadily westward and, more recently, taken a turn to the southwest.

Belle Fourche, South Dakota, geographic center of the fifty United States

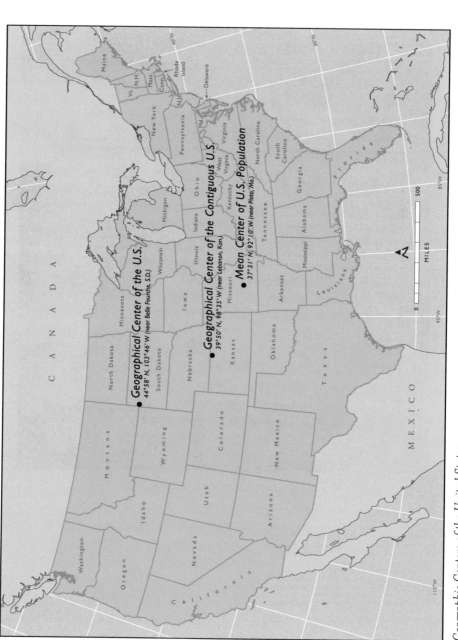

Geographic Centers of the United States

*   *   *

The tour book I had with me when I traveled to South America was written in Spanish and described the "Mapocho poderoso" (the powerful Mapocho River), and I looked forward to seeing it. I saw it almost daily for the better part of one year, but it was never very powerful. In fact, it wasn't much of a stream at all. The river flows through the center of Santiago, Chile. During the nineteenth century, a branch of the river was filled in and became the Avenida Liberator General Bernardo O'Higgins, the main street of the city, universally known as the Alameda. I wish I could say that the Mapocho is like the clean, pristine Seine that flows through Paris, but sadly, I cannot. The Mapocho is badly polluted by everything from raw sewage to tailings from copper mine operations upstream.

It is a bit ironic that I am writing this paragraph on the eighteenth of April, the date Longfellow used at the beginning of his poem about Paul Revere's ride. As generations of American schoolchildren learned, a signal was to be placed in the steeple of the Old North Church in Boston to let people know that the British were on the move. Their mission was to capture patriot leaders Samuel Adams and John Hancock, who were in Lexington, and to seize munitions that were stored at Concord. Paul Revere was one of several riders sent to warn Adams and Hancock as well as alert the countryside and the militia to the troop movement. We actually don't know all the riders, but William Dawes and Samuel Prescott (the only one to actually reach Lexington) deserve at least as much credit as Revere—but nobody wrote poems about them.

The lights (lanterns) in the church steeple appeared for only about a minute, but they were aimed at the opposite side of the Charles River, which flows through the center of Boston. Two lanterns were used, but there are three in existence claiming to be the two that were used. Amazing how valuable artifacts multiply!

* * *

New Spain was the principal holding of the Spanish in North America. At its zenith, it included Mexico and most of Central America, California, the Louisiana Territory, Florida, the Caribbean, a bit of South America, and even the Philippine Islands. Attempts to colonize the North American parts of New Spain initially went reasonably well. The establishment of missions, however, proved more difficult as settlements spread north into the region called the New Philippines. The natives proved more difficult to convert, and some were downright hostile to the Spanish. Moreover, the presence of the French in the lower Mississippi precluded much movement to the east. The missionaries named their principal mission in this area after St. Anthony (San Antonio) and eventually encouraged American settlement in the region. This they came to regret when the Americans drove the Mexican army out of the area.

General Santa Ana came back with three thousand troops to retake the New Philippines and surrounded the Americans at a mission designed to protect missionaries from Indian attack, not from attack by an army with cannons. People keep telling me to remember the name of the mission, but I just can't. I do know, however, that by this time the region was no longer the New Philippines, but rather Texas.

Dr. G. says: Santa Ana started toward the Alamo from San Luis Potosi with more than six thousand men, but he lost many along the way. By the time reinforcements arrived, he was estimated to have about three thousand men.

* * *

Anyone who has studied the Spanish language has probably encountered a fictional city with a central feature, the "Plaza de Armas." Such places do exist. There's one near the cathedral in Santiago, Chile, for example. In Mexico, however, even in relatively small cities, you often find that the central square is called the *zocalo* (with the accent on the first syllable). The first *zocalo*, not surprisingly, is in Mexico City. There, after overthrowing Spanish rule, the city decided to build a monument to independence. They built the base (*zocalo*) and never finished the rest. People began to refer to the center of the city by this word and, eventually, it became common usage for central squares all over the country.

Why do we Americans tell children (and believe it ourselves) that if we dig down through the earth, we'll reach China? If we actually could dig far enough, we'd come out on the floor of the Indian Ocean—unless, like me, you lived in Hawaii, in which case you'd come out in Botswana. Before you got to your destination, however, you'd encounter some interesting rock layers and, eventually, the core of the earth. Seismologists, those who send sound waves into the earth (or study vibrations from earthquakes), have concluded that the earth has an inner core and an outer core. The inner core, at the earth's center, is a dense solid, or at least something that acts like a solid, probably made of iron and nickel. The outer core is liquid. Since the earth continues to cool beneath our feet, portions of the outer core cool and solidify and join the inner core, or so the evidence indicates. Perhaps the strangest thing about the inner core is that it rotates slightly faster than the rest of the planet.

WORLD POPULATION

Question 104: At birth, what is most likely: a boy or a girl? Or are both equally likely to occur?

Question 105: What world region is growing the fastest?

Question 106: What region is losing the most population?

Question 107: What European country has lost the largest percentage of its population but is now the most rapidly growing?

Question 108: What Asian country is most threatened by population decline?

Over much of human history, population growth has been seen as a blessing. In even the most primitive economies, some degree of specialization of labor and, therefore, some minimum population size was necessary for survival. The exact size of that minimum would depend on the level of the economy as well as the richness of the environment from which resources were derived (e.g., animals to hunt, soil in which to plant). If that minimum survival number were not maintained, the group might perish. This was a significant problem because through most of mankind's existence, birth and death rates ran neck and neck. Strong pronatalist values (that is, values that favor childbearing) necessarily developed; women were expected to bear as many children as possible.

While "growth" is a word that has long been equated with prosperity, there have been times when population growth implied a threat. The first chapter in the biblical book of Exodus makes it clear that

Dr. G. says: Pronatalist values continue to exist today even though the conditions that originally fostered them have changed. Debates over abortion, birth control, sex education, "glass ceilings" in the workplace, and equal pay for equal work are all derived from these ancient values.

the growth of the slave class in ancient Egypt was seen as a threat. So was the crowding associated with the rapid growth of London in the late seventeenth and eighteenth centuries. By the end of the eighteenth century, Thomas Robert Malthus had written the first of his essays on population. He saw population as growing geometrically while food supply could grow only arithmetically; disaster was right around the corner! At the time he wrote, England's population was about 7.5 million, as compared with 53 million today.

During the 1960s, concern with population reached a near-fever pitch with the publication of numerous studies that once again raised the Malthusian dilemma, this time stressing resources in general, not just the food supply. Billions of dollars were spent on research and action programs to reduce birthrates. Unfortunately, the contributions of geographers and anthropologists were shoved into the background as population research increasingly was aimed at what was seen as a global crisis. Chapter 21 examines this issue in more detail.

Currently, more attention is being paid to the possibility of the shrinking of the world population rather than to its rapid growth. Several processes are under way to mitigate what otherwise would be dire consequences of population decline. Perhaps most importantly, global migration is almost certainly at historic highs. Areas that are more rapidly growing by an excess of births over deaths are providing migrants to areas that otherwise would be seeing their populations shrink. Some of the countries that showed the earliest symptoms of population decline are now showing at least a small rebound in birthrates and growth. While the global picture remains a bit murky, my prediction is that population decline will eventually replace global warming as the Popular Issue of the Day.

While common belief is that any given pregnancy has an equal chance of producing a boy or a girl, studies generally show that about 20 percent more boys are conceived than girls. At birth, the facts are firmly established and based on global data going back more than a century: there are approximately 5 percent more boys than girls. At age seventy-five, women outnumber men by about 25 percent in the United States and other developed countries. The facts concerning sex imbalance have apparently made researchers in biological and medical fields feel uncomfortable, probably because some postulates in genetics aver that males and females are equal in number at birth. This perhaps explains why so many studies have aimed at showing that sex imbalance is caused by environmental factors such as pollution and even global warming.

Geographers have focused their attention on areas where there are large imbalances—either way—in the sexes and have offered generalizations about why these imbalances exist. For example, frontier areas almost always have more men than women. The last two states admitted to the Union, Alaska and Hawaii, have both been male dominated for as long as reliable figures have been kept. In Hawaii's plantation days, men were imported as laborers initially; later military buildups in Hawaii produced an exceptionally large proportion of men between and during the world wars. The gold rush in the Yukon brought thousands of unaccompanied men north into Alaska as well as Canada. The United States as a whole has more women than men, but some areas, such as retirement areas in Florida, have especially large proportions of women.

On a world scale, South Asia (except Sri Lanka) and the Middle East along with China are the most prominent regions that have more men than women. The United Arab Emirates is the most "unbalanced" country in the world, with more than twice as many men as women. While local idiosyncratic reasons can be used to explain the sex ratio in parts of this broad region, both anthropologists and geographers have noted that boys are considered beneficial and girls a liability. My own students who have done fieldwork in parts of South Asia have noted that in some rural villages, boys are fed first, with girls receiving the food that is left over. In more urbanized settings, sonograms and sex-selective abortions are available, which may increase the proportion of males in the population.

The rate at which world population has been growing increased for several centuries (although not always consistently) and reached its maximum at around 1965; the growth rate, while still positive, has been declining since then. The areas with the current highest growth rates are in Africa and the Middle East. Growth rates have actually increased in a few sub-Saharan African regions since 1965 because modern medicine has been slow to move into some areas. As a result, death rates remained high, but as these few areas finally were affected by the introduction of immunizations and antibiotics, the falling death rates resulted in very rapid population growth.

Demographic projections extending beyond twenty-five years or so should be properly labeled as "guesses." The current guess by the US Census Bureau is that world population will be growing at about 0.5 percent annually by 2050. My guess is that world population will peak somewhat before 2050.

The region that has lost the most population is Eastern Europe. Bulgaria, Ukraine, Albania, Serbia, Estonia, and Belarus are among the countries with the highest rates of decline. Russia has probably lost the most population in total, but recent changes, especially the return of ethnic Russians from former Soviet territories, have stabilized the population. Putin's grab of the Crimea from Ukraine and his clear threats to areas of eastern Ukraine should be viewed as both demographically and geopolitically motivated. Russia's previously declining population appears to have been viewed by the Russian government as a real threat.

A second answer is possible to the question about regions of declining population. Several of the small Pacific island nations are experiencing sharp declines due to out-migration. The Federated States of Micronesia, for example, have agreements with the United States that permit free migration to US territory. Similarly, the Cook Islands are experiencing heavy out-migration to New Zealand. In percentage terms, these population losses are greater than in Eastern Europe but actually are quite small in terms of total numbers.

In 1841, the area that now constitutes the Republic of Ireland had a population of about 6.5 million. The potato had become a staple food of the Irish by 1720. A workman might consume sixty potatoes a day, a woman, forty. This dependence was on a single variety of potato called the Irish lumper. In the years 1739–41, potato crops were poor, and stored potatoes were destroyed by exceptionally cold weather. About one-eighth of the Irish population died in this famine. The famous potato blight, however, began in 1841. Approximately one million starved to death over the next few years, and another million left the country. By 1871, the population had declined to four million and continued to decline until 1926, when it reached three million and stabilized until the 1970s.

Dr. G. says: I know sixty potatoes per day seems high, but it is reported in several sources. A professor of nutrition at the University of Hawaii described the potato as the perfect food since, if you ate enough of them, you would ingest all the nutrients essential for life. He suggested that a large number need to be eaten to achieve this, but he did not go as far as sixty per day.

Since 1970, Ireland's population growth has been a real anomaly for a developed country. The most recent estimate is that the Irish population is growing at just under 2 percent per year. Currently, the Republic of Ireland has a population of about 4.6 million, up from its low point of 2.8 million in 1960. Ireland thus has the unique status of having fewer people than it did in 1841 and, at the same time, being the fastest-growing country in Europe. The real question is whether Ireland is a bellwether for Europe and perhaps the world: if global population declines, as it is expected to by mid-century (or later), can we then expect a rebound like Ireland's?

Many people picture Asia as possessing teeming cities and being threatened with overpopulation (whatever that means). Indeed, Japan's expansion in the 1930s into Manchuria and later into other parts of China was justified by its need for land for its expanding population—at least that was the Japanese government's excuse. Now Japan is threatened with a deep and sustained population decline. Its fertility is among the world's lowest and, while it has attempted to reclaim its citizenry that has emigrated, it is inconceivable that simple in-migration can mitigate population decline. By its traditions (bluntly!), Japan does not want immigrants. Its language, moreover, is unique to Japan, and there remains a residual (and ridiculous) belief in the notion that only Japanese can learn Japanese. How Japan deals with this slow but inevitable crisis is worth our attention because it is the same crisis that the world as a whole will eventually confront.

OTHER POPULATIONS

Question 109: What US state has the youngest population?

Question 110: What US state has the oldest median age?

Question 111: In what country does DNA evidence show that the men came from Norway and the women from Ireland?

Question 112: What country has the oldest average age of first marriage?

One of the things that make geography a useful scientific discipline is that geographers use their eyes and pay attention to real-world circumstances. This may seem, well, trivial at first, but scads of planning and economic development schemes have failed badly because of decision-making by people who knew next to nothing about the people or places they were planning for or "developing." My first experience with this was when I came upon a room of expensive, unused mainframe computer equipment in a hospital in Santiago, Chile, donated by US foreign aid. No one in the hospital had the slightest idea how to use the equipment, and those who did were not likely to go near the neighborhood where the hospital was located. My late colleague Dr. Donald Fryer used to alternate between fits of rage and howls of laughter over agricultural equipment designed to better cultivate and "modernize" rubber production in Malaysia—but was manufactured at a size considerably wider than the space between the rows of rubber tree plants.

A geographer encountering a village or small town for the first time sees the population. He probably does not know the birthrate or the death rate of the community, but he can see the ages and gender of the people. While he may not judge with perfect accuracy, still, what demographers call the age and sex structure of the community is visible to him. It is this visible feature of the community that can suggest the school-age population, the number of elderly, the size of the workforce, and other features that distinguish this particular place. Meanwhile, certain demographers and economic development specialists are trying their best to ignore the visible character of the population. Here's how it works:

Let's suppose USAID (US Agency for International Development) has spent twenty million dollars in developing a family planning program in Notopia aimed at reducing the high birthrate there. Eventually, Congress will ask USAID for a report on how well the program has done. A report is written, and it states: "In the three years since we spent the money, the birthrate of Notopia has dropped from thirty (births per thousand per year) to twenty-eight, so the money has been well spent." Unfortunately for USAID, a congressman on the Foreign Aid Committee actually knows something about birthrates (unlikely, I know, but this is a "let's suppose" story) and points out: "The number of Notopian women who are in the fifteen to forty-five age group, the ages in which almost all births occur, dropped substantially in the past three years, so even though the birthrate did go down, it went down only because there were fewer potential mothers. Our money had no influence."

USAID, chagrined that Congress would not accept its assurance, calls Professor Grant Seeker and asks him to develop some means of determining whether the family planning program is actually working. To do this, Dr. Seeker needs to filter out the influence of the age and sex structure on Notopia's population. He does this and publishes the results, whereupon other professors set to work devising even more sophisticated formulas to weed out the influence of age.

Unfortunately, USAID, Dr. Seeker, and those who follow in his footsteps are solving one problem in assessment while ignoring broader issues that may—and probably are—more important. The age structure of a population tells us a lot about the people within that population. An understanding of it helps us anticipate future needs: the number who will be seeking jobs in twenty years, or seeking to go to college, or looking for land to farm.

Here's a practical application of knowing about the age structure of a population that will help you keep your local politicians honest. Your mayor or police chief announces that property crime (theft, burglary) has gone down for five years in a row thanks to good police work. Property crime is committed by people of a variety of ages, but it is most likely to be committed by a fifteen-year-old. If the number of fifteen-year-olds has gone down in your community (which is the case in many American and European countries), property crime will go down. Good police work is to be commended, but it shouldn't be confused with the influence of age structure.

The youngest state in the United States by far is Utah, the only state with a median age of less than thirty. Trailing it are Texas and Alaska, both of which have had an influx of younger workers. The oldest state may come as a surprise. Maine has a median age of around forty-three and is followed closely by Vermont and West Virginia. Chances are you thought Florida or perhaps Arizona would have the oldest people; indeed, Florida does have the highest percentage of its population over sixty-five, but states with retirement communities attract a "shadow" population, people who migrate to provide services for the retired. Medical and dental services surround the retired, as do people serving the daily "early bird" special in restaurants. Many of these services employ younger people who have moved there because of the job opportunities. These younger people, of course, tend to lower the average age of the state's population. Maine is "old in place," that is, older because the population there has grown older, not because older people have moved in. Conversely, Florida is "old" because older people have moved there.

Cancer clusters or "hot spot" scares have occurred for decades. News reports describe an unusual number of deaths from cancer that have occurred in a small area, and speculation will grow about a problem with the water supply, the soil, or some other environmental factor. Confronted with this situation, public health officials first face the statistical problem of whether the number of cancer-related deaths is really high or whether the numbers can be considered a coincidence. After that, the problem becomes really difficult because both age and genetic factors can influence cancer. Cancer, particularly certain kinds of cancer, "runs in families." We may be able to control for age in a suspected "hot spot," but how can we control for genetic influences?

Let's imagine an isolated population that numbered around fifty thousand for a thousand-year period. Because the population is small and isolated (which implies that mate selection is made within the group of fifty thousand—no mail order brides or grooms), after the thousand years, you'd end up with a population that was literally homogeneous, that is, everyone would share a lot of genes in common. In other words, you'd have a wonderful population in which to study cancer "hot spots." Imagine no further! We have such a place, and it's called Iceland. Medical geographers have conducted such research in Iceland and, in the studies with which I am familiar, the hot spots have proved cold indeed. Exposure to certain chemicals and radiation can certainly cause cancer, but proving the presence and validity of cancer-causing hot spots is a true scientific challenge.

Iceland's genetics have proved ideal for other kinds of medical research as well, including DNA studies. Recent findings indicate that Icelandic men came from a Nordic population. The surprise was that Icelandic women came from a Gaelic population, almost certainly Ireland and the Faroe Islands. Historic sources suggest that early Icelandic wives were "thralls," slaves. The slave trade was an important part of the Viking economy, and Irish thralls were important in the early settlement of Iceland.

The Faroe Islands ought to elicit questions from students ("Is that where they built the pyramids?"), but they never did because I doubt whether anyone heard of them. The irony is that the islands actually look like pyramids, old volcanic structures rising out of the Atlantic. They were apparently stepping stones for early Gaelic residents of Iceland before the Vikings arrived. There are fewer than fifty thousand Faroese, but they are among today's most successful fish farmers. Swift currents supply salmon with a continuous supply of clean water.

A traditional Faroe Island house is black with a sod roof. Today, metal roofs predominate and offer protection against the intense winter storms. Some still prefer the sod roofs for an obvious reason: they're quieter during storms.

Sod-roofed house in the Faroe Islands

Dr. G. says: In the late 1990s, DNA research, especially in Iceland, was heralded as a medical breakthrough with enormous potential for new treatments and the elimination of gene-linked diseases. So far, the promise of this research has yet to be fulfilled.

*   *   *

In an earlier chapter, I noted that Ireland has fewer people today than it had at the middle of the nineteenth century. There are many reasons for that, but one fact that made Ireland stand out was the advanced age of marriage. Poverty and limited food supply were partially coped with by delaying marriage. Until fairly recently, in Western societies, almost all births occurred within marriage, so if marriage were postponed, the birthrate would be quite low regardless of other factors. Ireland stood out in that regard, since the median age of marriage was around thirty-five, the highest (or oldest) in the world. In comparison with the US population, Irish women married at an age at which American women had generally finished having children. This pattern has changed somewhat in recent years. American women are having children at somewhat older ages, and the Irish are marrying a bit younger. In fact, Ireland is now third in terms of marrying at an older age. Sweden is now first and Denmark, second: in all three countries, the average age of marriage is just under thirty-four.

DANGEROUS
WATERY PLACES

Question 113: The mouth of what river is between Cape Disappointment and Point Adams?

Question 114: What is known as "the graveyard of the Atlantic"?

Question 115: Who invented the lens used in modern lighthouses?

Question 116: Where is the only barber-pole (candy red and white helical striped) lighthouse in the United States?

Question 117: What famous naval battle took place in the Skagerrak?

Question 118: The French-owned Salvation Islands in the Caribbean contain Royale Island, St. Joseph Island, and what other famous island?

People have grown more sophisticated over time. Earlier advertising and political campaigns that once influenced people would be laughed at today. On the other hand, using a combination of modern psychology, graphs/statistics, and especially maps, it is easier to be convincing or to outright lie.

On the wall of my grandmother's house was a copy of a painting, *The Wreck of the Hesperus.* It was a fearful image with high waves, strong winds, and at least the suggestion of drowning sailors. I used to inwardly shudder every time I looked at it. I had no idea where the *Hesperus* had run into such trouble. Many years later, after my grandmother's house had become yet another abandoned house in a rural area, I ate lunch at a restaurant in Oregon. I received a paper placemat from the waitress and immediately noted that it was a map. The map depicted shipwrecks on the Oregon coast; there were so many that it took the entire meal to count them. Among them was the familiar name, *Hesperus*. This is proof positive that it is easier to lie with maps than with words. The wreck of the *Hesperus* was either a fictional account in a poem by Longfellow or an actual shipwreck; both occurred on the East Coast, Longfellow's version on the coast of Maine, or the real *Hesperus* that sank near Boston.

In the days when sailing ships ruled the oceans and long before satellite navigation, numerous places were highly dangerous. Ships were designed and built to withstand all but the heaviest weather; the real danger was that a ship would run into something. In certain places, currents were too strong for ships under sail to resist. In others, the prevailing winds would require a ship to come near a hazard. One of the world's most dangerous places was the mouth of the Columbia River, between Cape Disappointment and Point Adams. The entrance to the Columbia can be likened to a speed bump. Sand builds up from coastwise currents and then is redistributed by the flow of the river and tidal flow. One ship may make it through, but the following ship, taking the same route, may end up grounded and at the mercy of the currents. More than two thousand ships have been lost at the mouth of the Columbia, with more than seven hundred drownings.

The entrance to the Columbia River has been improved or at least changed in the past decade. Congress authorized additional dredging in the ship channel extending upriver from Astoria to Portland, Oregon. Improved aids to navigation over the years have made the mouth of the Columbia far less dangerous, but it remains the largest and most powerful river to empty into the Pacific from the Americas.

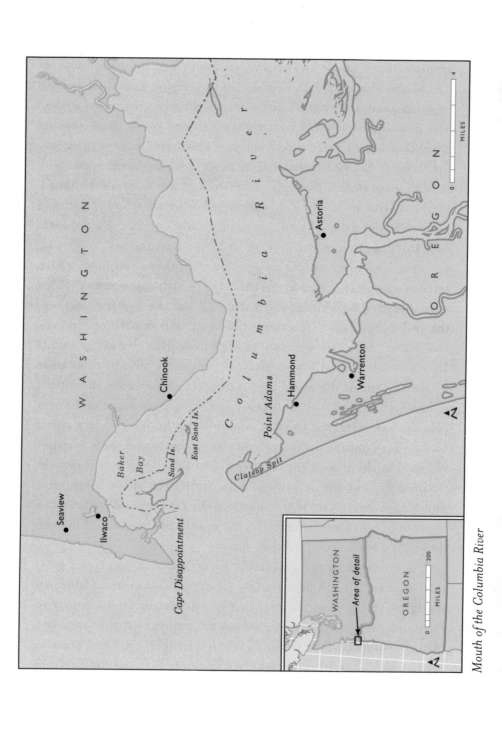

Mouth of the Columbia River

* * *

Remember the Sirens in Greek legend who would lure ships to their destruction? The real-life situation may be worse. Once aids to navigation were developed (some lighthouses date to ancient times), people discovered that they could build ersatz lighthouses and lure ships into shallows. Cargoes could be stolen in this way and sailors sold into slavery. Experienced captains sometimes placed no trust in lighthouses because of this danger and because, in some cases, the light, even if genuine, was often erratic.

One of the most famous lighthouses of all is at the area known as "the graveyard of the Atlantic," Cape Hatteras, North Carolina. At this point in the Atlantic, the cold Labrador Current and the warm Gulf Stream collide. This produces not only rough water but fog sufficient to obscure the Cape. An early lighthouse built there could not produce a beam strong enough to be of much use. In the mid-nineteenth century, a French scientist, Augustin-Jean Fresnel, developed a lens that was named after him. The Fresnel lens is based

Cape Hatteras, North Carolina, lighthouse moved to new location

on a concave lens but without most of the center, and what's left of the center is beveled. It produced much more light at Cape Hatteras. As far as I know, all lighthouses today use Fresnel lenses. Unfortunately, the shoreline at Hatteras began to recede, and in a massive operation the entire lighthouse was moved to a safer location.

Dr. G. says: I hate to do this to fans of Batman, but here goes. The famous searchlight that Commissioner Gordon uses to summon Batman—the one that projects an image of a bat in the sky—can't possibly exist. Only a searchlight with a Fresnel lens would be strong enough to do the job, but a Fresnel lens has no focal length, so it cannot possibly project an image. Let me assure you, however, that every other feature of the Batman stories is absolutely true.

* * *

Many aids to navigation have characteristics that allow their easy identification. A buoy, for example, may display a certain pattern of the light or a particular sound that it emits. Lighthouses, too, are often painted with a characteristic striping pattern that allows them to be identified in the daylight. The Cape Hatteras lighthouse is famous for its black spiral stripe. You would think that someone would design the outside of a lighthouse to look like a candy cane or barber pole. Someone did. The White Shoal lighthouse in Lake Michigan, about twenty miles west of the Mackinac Bridge, is painted in a red and white spiral, the only such design in the United States. This lighthouse also has "recon" capability, meaning that it has a transponder that picks up radar signals from ships and (here's an ultimate trivia question) sends back the letter "k" in Morse code.

The Skagerrak has accumulated hundreds of shipwrecks in the past, perhaps even more than the mouth of the Columbia River or Cape

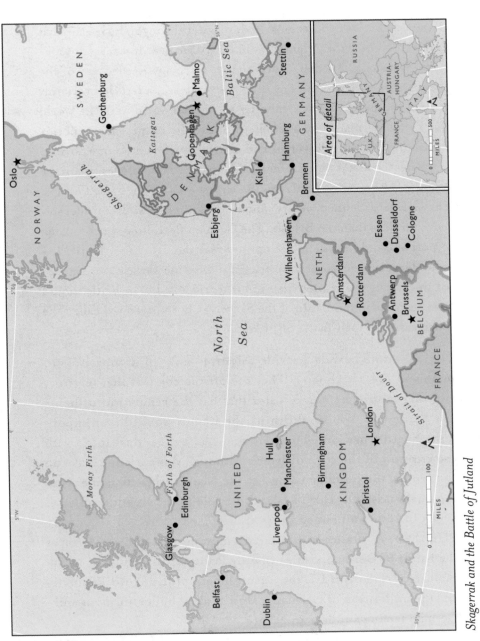

Skagerrak and the Battle of Jutland

Hatteras. This is the outermost body of water through which a ship has to travel to enter the Atlantic from the Baltic Sea. It is a strait separating Denmark, Sweden, and Norway. Germany needed use of the Skagerrak in order to put any of its vessels to sea, a fact that certainly did not escape Germany's enemies in the two world wars. In World War I, the German navy attempted to lure the numerically superior British fleet into the Skagerrak and destroy a sufficiently large portion of the fleet so that it would later be able to put its own battleships in the Atlantic. The ensuing battle was the largest ever fought by battleships. The Germans claimed victory, and they did indeed sink considerably more tonnage than the British. The German fleet, however, returned to port and did not again attempt to break out into the Atlantic. Instead, Germany declared unrestricted submarine warfare, a main factor in drawing the United States into World War I. The battle should have been called the Battle of the Skagerrak but instead was called the much easier to spell Battle of Jutland.

The Salvation Islands provide salvation only in comparison to mainland French Guiana. They are off the coast of that territory and surrounded by murky water that has the reputation of being shark infested. You would think the islands would be unimportant. As it turned out, however, they had a great deal to do with the creation of the state of Israel. Although three islands make up the group, the popular name for the islands takes its name from the smallest island: Devil's Island. Its role in the creation of Israel began in 1894 and ended in 1906.

In 1870–71, France had suffered a monumental military defeat at the hands of German armies (mostly Prussian) that resulted in the capture of Napoleon III, the establishment of the Third Republic, and the unification of Germany. Most of all, it built enormous anti-German feeling and fear in France.

In 1896, a French army officer named Alfred Dreyfus was convicted in a secret court martial of giving French military secrets to the German Embassy in Paris. Dreyfus was Alsatian, from an area

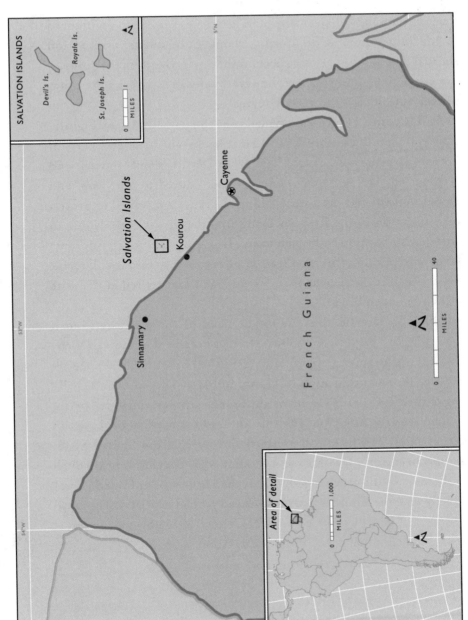

Salvation Islands

Kourou

Cayenne

Sinnamary

French Guiana

0   MILES   40

Area of detail

0   MILES   1,000

Salvation Islands

that was then part of Germany, and he was Jewish. He was sentenced to life imprisonment on Devil's Island. Subsequent investigation showed that another army officer, rather than Dreyfus, was guilty of the crime. The French army, however, refused to convict the other officer but did agree to retry Dreyfus.

At this point, France was divided over the Dreyfus Affair. Significant anti-Semitic outbreaks and riots broke out in several parts of France. Dreyfus was brought back from Devil's Island, retried, and reconvicted. His sentence, however, was reduced to ten years, and he was immediately pardoned. Many in France continued to protest his conviction in the first place, arguing that it was entirely due to anti-Jewish bias in the French army. In 1906, the French Supreme Court ordered Dreyfus exonerated and restored to his rank. Dreyfus fought against the Germans in World War I and retired at the rank of lieutenant colonel.

Although Dreyfus died in 1935, many of those in the French army who had been strongly anti-Dreyfus became the rulers of Vichy France, the German puppet state established in southern France after the German occupation of France in 1940. They were quite willing to turn over to the Germans any French citizens who were Jewish.

The Dreyfus Affair put life into the Zionist movement, based in Switzerland. Many Jews in Western Europe and the United States saw no need for a Jewish state, but after what Dreyfus went through in France, opinions changed. When the Holocaust unfolded, it was exactly what the Zionists had most feared yet had expected. The 1948 creation of Israel by vote of the UN General Assembly was, in a real sense, the culmination of the Dreyfus Affair.

FORCED MIGRATION

Perhaps the greatest forced migration in world history was the movement of enslaved Africans across the Atlantic Ocean. I have seen several conflicting estimates of the total number involved, which is understandable since the destination of Africans included such a vast territory. Certainly millions were involved. There were, however, many other forced migrations in history, perhaps not of the scale of the transatlantic migration, but each important in its own right and each of great significance to the people affected.

The Native American peoples that lived in the southeastern United States had been urged to adopt "modern" ways by numerous American leaders, including George Washington. That seems to have been what was happening in the fifty years following American independence. In one of the most remarkable events in linguistics, a Cherokee named Sequoyah invented a syllabary (not an alphabet) for the Cherokee language. He first tried a system similar to hieroglyphics in which symbols represented ideas, but this required too much memorization. Then he hit on an idea that was superior to the alphabet, a system of eighty-six syllables represented by symbols. While convincing the Cherokees to accept it was almost as difficult as the invention itself, once it was accepted, it spread rapidly. Cherokees, using their system, could learn to read and write in a matter of weeks, while an alphabetic system usually takes two years of instruction. The Cherokees, by 1830, probably had a higher level of literacy than the whites living in the area.

Dr. G. says: Probably you know that the giant California tree is named for this Cherokee, but beyond that, it is not possible to say much about Sequoyah. There are different ideas about his background, and benchmarks in his life that nineteenth-century scholars accepted have now been challenged as "myths."

The so-called Five Civilized Tribes (Cherokee, Choctaw, Muscogee/Creek, Chickasaw, and Seminole) had adopted many white practices, but in a series of actions beginning in the 1830s, the US government forcibly removed them from their land in the southeastern United States and assigned them to land in the Indian Territory (roughly, the present state of Oklahoma). Thousands died in the trek. If you considered this entire movement to be the "Trail of Tears," I'll generously give you credit for a correct answer. The term, however, seems to have originally referred to the movement of only the Cherokee, who had farther to move and less time to prepare. President Martin Van Buren's edict meant that more than one-third of the Cherokee who moved perished on the way.

* * *

You probably know that when British India gained its independence in 1947, it was partitioned into two countries based on religion: India, Hindu and Sikh, and Pakistan, Islam. You may also know that "religion" did not necessarily mean the religion of the majority of the people living in an area but rather the religion of whomever was ruling the area. You may not know, however, that today, India has the third-largest Muslim population of any country, with about 120 million Muslims. The process of granting independence produced an enormous problem that was partially a result of the haste of British authorities in dealing with the partition issue. Sir Cyril Radcliffe, who had never been to India, was given responsibility for drawing the line that divided India and Pakistan, and the line between the countries was thus called the "Radcliffe Line." Radcliffe was given just five weeks to complete the job with not even a geographer to advise him.

Since much of the partition was to be between already-existing political subdivisions, the real difficulty arose over the need to divide two large provinces: Punjab and Bengal. Radcliffe's division went through the middle of large communities, through villages, and sometimes through existing houses. Once independence was declared, there seemed to be genuine surprise at what happened: an estimated fourteen million people decided to move to the other side of the Radcliffe Line, probably the largest migration in recent times. Since Muslims were moving one way and Hindus another, they met along the way and killed each other; an estimated one million people died, either directly from sectarian violence or from the hardship of the journey. The British were gone and took no responsibility, while neither new government had found the time to regulate the migration or mitigate the violence.

Bizet's opera *Carmen* was not well received when it was first performed in Paris. The main problem was that the principal characters were all killed during the opera, something we now accept as common in many

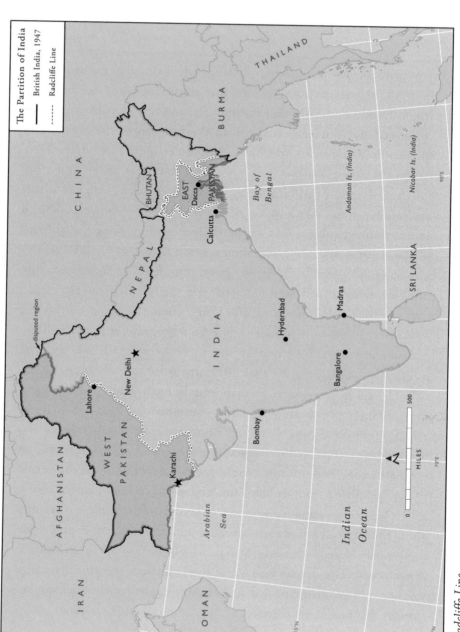

The Partition of India

British India, 1947
Radcliffe Line

CHINA

THAILAND

BURMA

BHUTAN

NEPAL

EAST
Dacca
PAKISTAN

Calcutta

Bay of
Bengal

Andaman Is. (India)

Nicobar Is. (India)

disputed region

Lahore

New Delhi

INDIA

Hyderabad

Madras

AFGHANISTAN

WEST
PAKISTAN

Bangalore

SRI LANKA

Karachi

Bombay

Arabian
Sea

IRAN

OMAN

Indian
Ocean

MILES

500

0

Radcliffe Line

Vincent van Gogh, Encampment of Gypsies with Caravan

movies and TV shows, but which horrified French operagoers and reviewers at the time. The title character, Carmen, was a gypsy, a term that is now considered derogatory. Carmen would more properly be called Romani or some variation of that term. These people, known for their exclusiveness and nomadism, were probably called "Gypsies" because people thought they came from Egypt, but they didn't. They actually came from North India and migrated westward into Europe as early as the twelfth century. The Romanis were victims of Hitler's plans for elimination of "undesirables" from the German population. In 1935, they were stripped of German citizenship and thereafter sent to extermination camps. Since Romanis were never counted as a separate group in European censuses, it is impossible to know how many died in what the Romanis call the *porajmos,* the equivalent of the Jewish Holocaust. Estimates run as high as 1.5 million. Following World War

II, the Romanis were subject to a eugenics law in Czechoslovakia in which women were to be sterilized because of their high birthrates. More recently still, since 2010 the Italian government has considered the Romanis a "security threat," while France has deported a small number after destroying a Romani encampment.

At the time of the Reformation in Europe, John Calvin influenced French Protestants who formed the French Reformed Church. For reasons still debated, these Protestants became known as Huguenots. They were a small minority in France, but their influence outweighed their numbers. Some were nobles, others were skilled craftsmen or artisans, and some were early capitalists whose entrepreneurship was vital to France.

In 1572, in what is called the St. Bartholomew's Day Massacre (it actually lasted over a month), thousands of Huguenots were slaughtered in Paris and elsewhere by Catholic mobs. In 1598, Henry IV proclaimed the Edict of Nantes, which promised religious freedom (with some small print) in France. The Huguenots again thrived in this atmosphere.

Under the rule of Louis XIV, France achieved a word geopoliticians love: hegemony. Militarily and economically, France was the world leader. One wag noted that Louis's palace at Versailles probably weighed more than all the buildings in New York City at the time. Even relations with England were good. In 1685, however, Louis was persuaded that the fate of his soul depended on doing something about the heretical Huguenots. He issued the Edict of Versailles, which required the conversion of the Huguenots to Catholicism. In fact, about three-quarters of the Huguenots complied, but many of those who converted were part of the rural peasantry. Those Huguenots, who could afford to, fled the country, thus depriving France of an important middle class. This has been called Europe's first "brain drain," and ultimately it destroyed France's hegemony so that even Napoleon Bonaparte could not restore it fully. Louis XIV was no longer trusted by the Protestant countries that were his major rivals; some have called the ensuing struggle with England "the second Hundred Years' War."

Dr. G says: New Paltz, New York, was one of the earliest
Huguenot settlements in the United States.

*   *   *

While large numbers of the Five Civilized Tribes were eventually
moved to Oklahoma, one of them had earlier fled the encroachment
of the white man and moved south into Florida. Before it became
part of the United States, Florida had been ruled by Spain and Great
Britain, and the tribe had reached at least an accommodation with
colonial authorities. The Spanish referred to the group as *cimarrones*,
or "runaways," since they had originally been from the Creek nation in the Carolinas; "Seminoles" is the corruption of the original
Spanish term.

When the United States took possession of Florida in 1818, it began to wage a war against the Seminoles that would last thirty years. A
few Seminoles escaped and have remained in Florida to this day. Not
all the Seminoles were American Indians. Some were Africans who
escaped from South Carolina; they spoke the low-country Gullah, an
African creole spoken from North Carolina to Florida. The Florida
Seminoles claim—and they may be right—that they are the only American Indians who never surrendered to the US government.

FORBIDDEN PLACES

Question 124: What is the "forbidden island" in the Hawaiian Islands?

Question 125: Where is the Forbidden City?

Question 126: What country, generally forbidden to Americans, receives about two million tourists annually?

Question 127: What country has a thirty-kilometer zone of alienation in which people are not allowed?

Question 128: What country, sharing a border with Russia, has an "eternal president" who, despite being eternal, died some time ago?

Question 129: Where is North Brother Island, where Typhoid Mary was held in quarantine (1907–10 and 1915–38)?

The village in which I grew up had a number of beautiful churches on its main street. They are mostly gone now, replaced first by gas stations and then by fast-food dispensaries. When I was quite small, I would ask my mother and father why we always went to the same church—some of the others were considerably bigger and more beautiful. I never got a straight answer, but I got the idea that these were Forbidden Places for me, mysterious and real curiosities. This proved to be an irony, for by the time I reached fifth grade, the school ran out of classroom space. I spent the next three school years going to all these different churches since they rented out rooms to the school district. The charm of these forbidden places soon faded. Forbidden places today conjure up the same sense of mystery and curiosity that the churches used to have for me.

Niihau Island, Hawaii

Actually, a number of islands in the Hawaiian chain are forbidden for most uses. The Northwest Hawaiian Islands, extending from Kauai to Kure Atoll, are a national marine and wildlife sanctuary and are accessible only by permit. Within the main, settled group of Hawaiian Islands, a portion of one island, Molokai, now open to visitors, was once considered one of the most forbidden places in the world. A peninsula jutting out from the sea cliffs on the north shore was home to the leper (Hansen's disease) colony there. One entire island, however, Niihau, is often called the forbidden island because it is privately owned by the Robinson family and accessible only with their permission. Niihau is home to about 120 people, and the Hawaiian language is spoken as the first language there.

Dr. G. says: One story, commonly told in Hawaii, is that Niihau really became "forbidden" when polio broke out in Honolulu and all travel to Niihau was curtailed.

In a rare burst of insight, the US government in the 1930s thought the Japanese might seize the flat island, Niihau, and use it as an air base to attack Pearl Harbor or as an emergency landing field for crippled planes following an attack. So in a highly secret mission, a landowner dug deep furrows across Niihau to prevent planes from landing. On December 7, 1941, a Japanese plane that had participated in the attack on Pearl Harbor did, in fact, land on Niihau. The pilot was eventually captured and killed.

The Forbidden City was the capital of China during the Ming and Qing (Manchu) dynasties. It was said to be "forbidden" because one

Forbidden City, Beijing, China

could enter it only with the permission of the emperor. It covers an area of over 150 acres in the center of Beijing, China. Prior to the building of the Forbidden City, China had been an active naval and exploratory power and had established settlements and influence in several parts of Asia. With time, China likely would have crossed the Pacific and perhaps established a settlement in the Americas before the Europeans. The Ming dynasty, however, brought a period of isolation, and exploration ceased. In contemporary China, the Forbidden City features a controversial Starbucks.

The Spanish-American War began in Cuba in 1898 with the sinking of the US battleship *Maine* and the loss of nearly three hundred American sailors. To this day (and despite an investigation one hundred years later by *National Geographic*), no one can be sure whether the *Maine* was sunk by a Spanish mine or whether an accidental explosion was the cause. If it was an accident, it was most unfortunate for Spain because it set the American press and public on the warpath. America's global naval power threatened Spain in Cuba, in the Philippines, and in Spain itself. When Spain finally sued for peace, the remnants of the Spanish Empire disappeared: Guam, Puerto Rico, the Philippines, and Cuba passed into American hands.

Cuba remained under direct US control only until 1902, when the Republic of Cuba was established. The Cuban constitution, however, granted the United States the power to intervene in Cuba and to control its foreign policy. In fact, over the next fifty years, the United States exerted strong influence over Cuba, and as late as the 1950s it was said that the US ambassador to Cuba was second in power and authority only to the president (or dictator) of Cuba.

In 1959, the government of Fulgencio Batista was overthrown by a group known as the 26th of July Movement. Fidel Castro became the "administrator" of Cuba. There was a great deal of discussion in the United States about whether or not Castro was a communist or whether he was hostile to the United States. Eventually, the Eisenhower administration decided Castro must be overthrown and began planning for the unsuccessful Bay of Pigs invasion. Sanctions against Cuba by the United States have remained in place to the present and have turned Cuba into a forbidden place for Americans. Although travel restrictions have been slightly eased (and frequently broken), Cuba remains strangely forbidden, while Cuba's closest ally, China, is open to Americans. Tourism, once discouraged by the Castro regime, has now begun to grow and is already a significant contributor to the economy.

Dr. G. says: Very recently Cuba and the United States have renewed diplomatic relations. This may end the trade boycott and permit American tourists to visit Cuba.

*   *   *

During the Cold War, the American public was conditioned to be terribly afraid of everything to do with "nukes" and radiation. Schoolchildren were taught to crawl under their desks in school, and "airplane spotters" were trained with the idea that attacking bombers could fly underneath radar detection. At the same time as this was going on, the United States was beginning to build nuclear reactors that could generate electricity. It was hard to be deathly afraid of something and at the same time embrace something with the same name that was supposed to safely produce electricity. Not surprisingly, Americans have always been dubious about the safety of nuclear power plants.

Dr. G. says: When my landlady (while I was a college student) learned that her electricity might come from a nearby nuclear power plant, she refused to change burned-out lightbulbs!

Nevertheless, nuclear energy promised to be the answer to shrinking supplies of fossil fuels and the pollution they generated along with electricity. France became highly dependent on nuclear-generated electricity, as did the United Kingdom and Japan. Approximately one hundred nuclear reactors provide electricity in the United States, 10 percent of the number anticipated by the Atomic Energy Commission in the 1950s. No new reactors have been opened in the United States since 1974. Currently plans are under way to build five more reactors and to close about six existing reactors. The United States produces more electricity by nuclear generator than any other country, but it still accounts for less than 20 percent of the electricity produced in the country.

Much of the world's attitude toward nuclear power was changed in April 1986 with the disaster at the Chernobyl facility in the USSR. It is hard to call what happened there an accident since the explosion and fire were caused by an experimental procedure that produced a power surge that essentially rendered the plant incapable of being cooled. Initial reports and subsequent official studies are enough to boggle the mind. Even the most basic information is directly contradicted in each new study. No Homer Simpson script could possibly match what actually happened.

A radius of thirty miles around the disaster site at Chernobyl is officially called the "zone of alienation." Originally, no one was to be allowed into this area, literally a forbidden place. Unbelievably, however, around three hundred people refused to leave and continue to live within the forbidden zone.

Most people forget (or perhaps never knew) that North Korea shares a border with Russia. North Korea is a forbidden place to most people, especially Americans, since the North Korean regime considers itself to be still in a state of war with the United States. Long before there was a country called North Korea, the Korean peninsula was called "the Hermit Kingdom" and attempted to isolate itself from the two stronger countries that surrounded it: Japan and China. Maintaining cultural and racial purity through isolation was the way Korea chose to enable it to survive. North Korea's isolation from the rest of the world, then, is a continuation, albeit an exceptional one, of Korea's ancient survival strategy.

Kim Il-Sung became the leader of North Korea shortly after Korea was divided north and south along the thirty-eighth degree of north latitude; the division was agreed upon by the United Nations after World War II. The Kim family has continued to rule North Korea ever since, with the present dictator, a grandson of Kim Il-Sung, taking power in 2011. Even in death, Kim Il-Sung is now revered as "eternal president" of North Korea.

Because North Korea depends on foreign aid and especially food imports for survival, and because it is distant from most of the United States, Americans tend to take North Korea's saber-rattling as somewhat humorous. The reality is quite different. While North Korea probably does not unilaterally have the capability of carrying out a sustained war, it has perhaps the largest army in the world, capable with full mobilization of putting eight million men under arms. It also has the largest submarine fleet in the world as well as nuclear weapons and a growing ability to deliver them by long-range missiles.

North Brother Island is a small island in New York's East River. It was uninhabited until 1885, when Riverside Hospital was relocated there as an isolation area for smallpox patients. Today, it is a bird sanctuary, again uninhabited and forbidden to the public.

Mary Mallon was quarantined on North Brother Island for much of her life. She was the first person identified as an asymptomatic carrier of typhoid fever. Mallon, who came to be called "Typhoid Mary," worked as a cook in the New York area and infected members of the households in which she worked. She adamantly refused to cooperate with health officials. After being quarantined on North Brother Island for three years, officials agreed to release her if she promised to never again work as a cook and to practice washing her hands (which she had resisted up to that point). After her release, however, she again became a cook and again began starting typhoid outbreaks. It was difficult to track her down since she had learned to change jobs and her name as soon as typhoid broke out. Eventually she was caught and returned to North Brother Island. When she died, North Brother Island was abandoned and is now covered with a heavy forest.

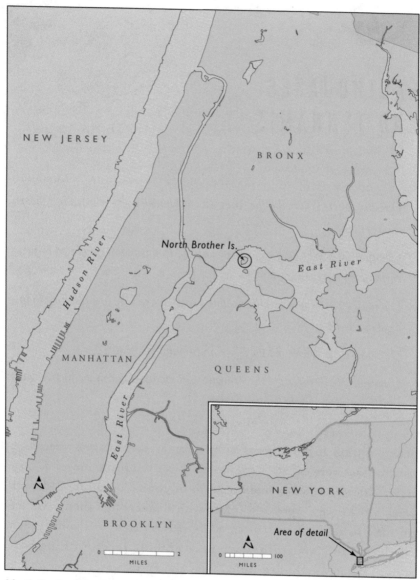

North Brother Island

EARTHQUAKES
AND TSUNAMIS

Question 130: Where did the strongest earthquake ever recorded by modern devices occur?

Question 131: What US city was devastated by a tsunami generated by the earthquake in Question 130?

Question 132: Where was the deadliest earthquake (the one resulting in the most deaths)?

Question 133: Where did the "orphan tsunami" originate?

Question 134: Where did the strongest earthquake occur in the forty-eight contiguous states of the United States?

When I took my first geography course, ocean waves created by earthquakes were called "tidal waves." Over the years, however, "tsunami" increasingly became the term of choice, and those who still used "tidal waves" were told (often with a sneer) that such waves had nothing to do with the tides. While this is true, "tsunami" means "harbor wave," and such waves have nothing to do with harbors, either. Whatever they're called, the power of waves generated by earthquakes can be worse than the earthquakes themselves. Witness the nuclear reactor at Fukushima, Japan, that was built to withstand earthquakes (and did) but was destroyed by a tsunami.

A TV quiz program asked the question, "What country is most threatened by earthquake?" and proposed the answer, "Japan."

While this is not an unreasonable answer, many other countries might qualify, depending on how "threatened" is defined. At a minimum, "threat" has to include both the strength of the earthquake and its location relative to human populations. New Zealand and Chile are frequently visited by earthquakes, but both have relatively low population densities, especially compared with Japan. Japan, however, has anticipated earthquakes for centuries and constructed buildings accordingly, while rural areas of China, Iran, and Turkey can suffer heavy loss of life from even modest quakes, often because their structures are both massive and highly vulnerable. Another factor to take into account is the ability to recover from earthquake damage. Again, Japan can respond quickly to most earthquakes, while Haiti, the poorest country in the Western Hemisphere, may require decades, even with massive external aid, to recover from the quake that devastated its capital, Port au Prince.

When my family and I lived in Chile, our landlady told us that her cousin and his wife were driving near the Chilean coast on May 22, 1960, when, seemingly in an instant, they were no longer on the mainland but on a small island that contained no more than one hundred meters or so of the road on which they had been driving. Several days passed before they were rescued. They managed to live through the strongest earthquake ever recorded, the Valdivia (Chile) earthquake. At least three significant quakes had struck the southern vale of Chile a few days before "the big one" hit, but they had been centered in rural areas near Lake Llanquihue and Lake Todos los Santos. The official reports on death and damage have remained vague to this day, with the death toll estimated at between three thousand and six thousand. Both my landlady and other Chileans with whom I worked claimed that the death toll was much higher, but that because entire families and their friendship networks had been killed, no one was left alive to report the deaths (or mourn for the dead).

Dr. G. says: Too often information reaches historians through rumor, or government intelligence officers rely on reports made by taxi drivers taking them to their hotels. The information I report here could be in that same vein. Still, having seen some of the official reports and knowing that those reports tell of whole villages disappearing with "unknown" loss of life, I think my landlady and those who shared her views may be reporting the best information available.

* * *

The Valdivia quake generated local tsunamis that did considerable damage, but the main wave traveled westward across the Pacific and devastated Hilo, Hawaii. Despite some advance warning, more than five hundred buildings were destroyed in downtown Hilo, and sixty-one people died.

Hilo suffered even more tsunami damage in 1946, when more than ninety people were killed. That tsunami was especially notori-

Hilo, Hawaii, tsunami strikes, 1946

ous for having taken the lives of schoolchildren at Laupahoehoe, a few miles north of Hilo on the island of Hawaii. The children and some of their teachers were astonished to see that the ocean fronting their school had suddenly become dry land and walked out to see what was going on. A series of returning waves swept the victims away.

It is possible that Hilo is the most threatened city in the United States, somewhat by earthquake, somewhat by tsunami, and somewhat by tropical hurricane, but mostly by Mauna Loa volcano. An eruption there (probably overdue) could wipe Hilo off the map if the lava flowed in the direction of the city.

The two candidates for the most deadly earthquake of all time both occurred in historical times, so the death tolls are somewhat speculative. The US Geological Survey cites the Shaanxi, China, earthquake of January 23, 1556, as the worst. It is believed that more than 830,000 people were killed in this quake. The competitor for most deadly occurred in the eastern end of the Mediterranean on July 5, 1201, and affected an area extending from Egypt to Syria. Compounding this event was a second powerful earthquake that struck Syria about ten months later. The estimated death toll, both directly from the two quakes and from disease and starvation in the quakes' aftermath, was about 1,100,000.

Early in the year 1700, a tsunami hit the coast of Japan. There were no reports of earthquakes, however, anywhere in the Pacific Basin. Since its source was unknown, it became known as the "orphan tsunami." Evidence gathered later from several sources identified the Cascadia earthquake, a massive quake, as the culprit. The earthquake zone extended from the northern end of Vancouver Island in British Columbia to Northern California. Perhaps the most disturbing thing about the Cascadia earthquake was that geologic evidence pointed to quakes occurring along the same fault line every four hundred to six hundred years.

While predicting earthquakes with any degree of accuracy is a future hope, it is worth considering that while there were no urban centers in the area of the Cascadia quake in 1700, there are now cities like Seattle, Victoria, and Vancouver. While tsunami damage is possible in these cities from a massive earthquake, direct damage from the quake itself is more likely. Many of the structures in these cities were built before the Cascadia quake and its predecessors were known and therefore are more vulnerable than buildings in Japan or San Francisco.

Because it is so famous, the San Francisco earthquake is often assumed to be the most powerful to have hit the continental United States. Instead, however, we have to look in a surprising place. Geomorphologists who study North American landforms refer to the "stable interior" of the continent. While a lot of earthquakes occur on the Pacific Coast and a few on the East Coast (for example, the one that recently damaged the Washington Monument in Washington, DC), quakes are relatively rare in the interior. An exception to this is a fault line near the Mississippi River, often called the New Madrid (Missouri) seismic zone. This zone began to generate a series of quakes in December 1811 and culminated in a huge quake centered on New Madrid in February 1812. New Madrid itself was destroyed, damage to some structures occurred in St. Louis, and church bells rang due to the shocks felt as far away as New York and Boston.

Dr. G. says: Geomorphology is the study of landforms, while geology is actually the study of the earth's history.

The New Madrid earthquake has been estimated as a magnitude 8 based on the damage done: it generated a wave in the Mississippi River that caused the river to flow northward, waterfalls were created in the Mississippi, and a new lake was generated.

Dr. G. says: When an earthquake occurs in the United States, the typical news story will report "a magnitude x on the Richter scale." I have not personally read a newspaper account of an earthquake in which the reporter realized two critical things: (1) the Richter scale was replaced by the moment magnitude scale (MMS) in most of the world more than thirty years ago, and (2) both scales are logarithmic to the base 10, meaning that a magnitude 6 quake is ten times greater than a 5, a magnitude 7 quake is one hundred times greater than a 5, and so on. Up to magnitude 7, both Richter and the MMS scale yield similar results; above 7, the Richter scale is essentially useless.

EXTREME POINTS

Question 135: What is the highest point on earth measured from the earth's center?

Question 136: Where is the world's highest settlement?

Question 137: Where is the highest settlement in the United States?

Question 138: What country has 20 percent of its land and 21 percent of its population below sea level?

Question 139: Where and what is Point Nemo?

Question 140: What is the most remote city of at least 500,000 population?

Of course, everyone knows Mt. Everest is the highest mountain on earth; seemingly someone climbs it or dies in the attempt about once a week. But wait a minute—is it really the highest mountain? We measure mountain height from sea level, but what if we measured from the center of the earth? After all, Al Gore lets us know at every opportunity that sea level is rising, and that has the net effect of lowering the height of every mountain (unless the mountains are still growing, as some are). Why not measure mountain height from the center of the earth? That's a stable point, not subject to the constantly changing level of the oceans.

The earth is not perfectly round but bulges a bit at the equator, which means that a high mountain very close to the equator is likely to be farther from the earth's center than Mt. Everest. We can find

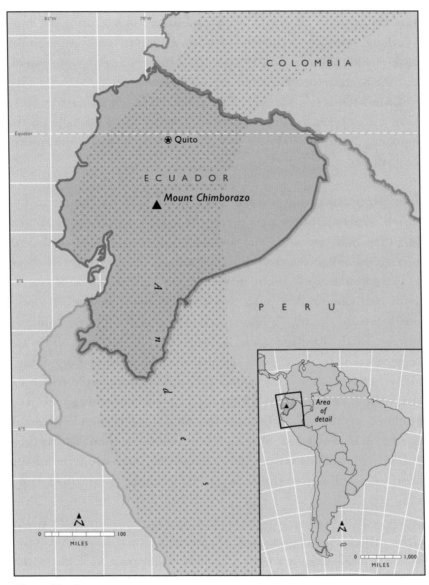

Mount Chimborazo

this mountain in Ecuador, Mt. Chimborazo, which, using the conventional measure, is only 20,564 feet above sea level, not even the highest mountain in South America using sea level measurement, but the peak farthest from the earth's center.

Chimborazo is a volcano, but it has not been active for more than 1,500 years. It is also glaciated, despite being virtually on the equator, and the glacial melt provides water for several communities downslope.

It is astonishing what a small space in the universe man can call home. Only about 30 percent of the earth's surface is land, and less than half the land can support more than a few people. We often overlook the vertical dimension to all this: from sea level, we can live upward only about three miles or so. There are, however, a few settlements that push this atmospheric envelope. Without much serious doubt, La Rinconada, Peru, is the highest community on earth. La Rinconada is more than 16,700 feet above sea level, more than three times the altitude of the "Mile-High City," Denver. Surprisingly, more than thirty thousand people live in La Rinconada, and not surprisingly, they have a compelling reason to be there: a gold mine. The fact that this is the highest settlement in the world is attested to by no less an authority than *National Geographic*. Experienced trivia players know that the nationality of the host often influences the answer. For example, a Brazilian running a trivia game will insist that the Amazon is the longest river in the world (and it may be) while others insist the Nile is the right answer. An Asian master of ceremonies may insist that Wenquan, China, is the highest settlement rather than La Rinconada. Wenquan is at only 16,467 feet above sea level, but its status as the world's highest settlement is listed in the *Guinness Book of World Records*. No gold mine in Wenquan; it is apparently a collection of a few buildings providing services to the road and railroad connecting China proper to Tibet.

Alma, Colorado, 1870s, highest settlement in the United States

* * *

As I write this paragraph, I am less than fifteen miles from the highest settlement in North America, Alma, Colorado. Alma was incorporated in 1873 and is just slightly less than 10,600 feet above sea level. In this case, it was not gold but silver that was responsible for the settlement. Colorado and many other places worldwide have gold and other valuable ores that are too expensive to mine at the moment. Often these mines have extracted metals from all their high-grade ore, but it would take a significant and sustained increase in commodity prices to bring most of these mines back into production.

It is certainly possible for inland communities to live below sea level, but living below sea level at the *edge* of the sea is more challenging. Lands that have been reclaimed from swamps or the sea are called polders. While polders are found in many countries, they are commonly associated with the Netherlands, where one-fifth of the coun-

Polder pumping station, Netherlands

try's land and population is below sea level. The first Dutch polders were built in the eleventh century and have become more numerous and much more sophisticated over the centuries. Today there are more than three thousand polders in the Netherlands.

The science (hydrology) involved with maintaining the polder lands comes close to being a scientific miracle. Storms in the North Sea, river floods, heavy rainfall, and even droughts (which can cause shrinkage of the ground) all have to be taken into account. The Dutch are well aware that sea level is rising, and the rate of change is likely increased by climate change. The Dutch are not the most threatened by rising sea levels (I would nominate Tuvalu and the Andaman Islands), but they are among the most active in anticipating it.

Point Nemo is found at 48 degrees, 52 minutes, 6 seconds south latitude and 123 degrees, 23 minutes, 6 seconds west longitude. This point is also called the oceanic pole of inaccessibility, and it is the point farthest from land. Point Nemo is in the South Pacific,

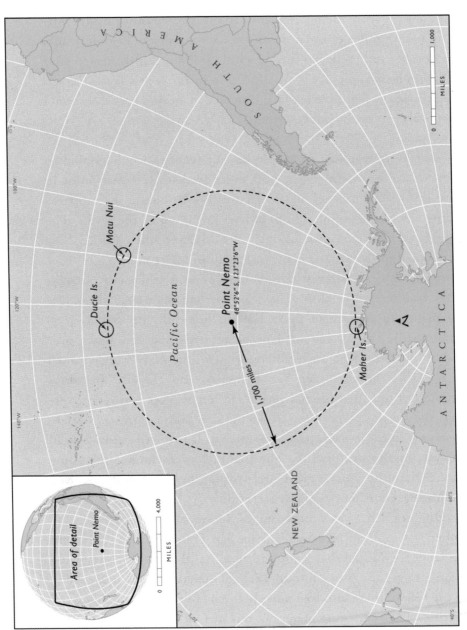

Point Nemo

1,670 miles from the nearest land, and it is surrounded by 8.5 million square miles of open ocean—not a good place, I would think, to discover your boat has sprung a leak. It is apparently named after Captain Nemo, captain of the *Nautilus* in Jules Verne's *Twenty Thousand Leagues under the Sea*. Exactly why it is so named escapes me . . . I should probably reread the book.

A surprising number of people do not realize that the Hawaiian Islands are approximately 2,500 miles from the nearest point in the continental United States. That makes Honolulu the most remote city with a population of at least 500,000 in the world. The degree of remoteness was dramatically displayed when the US Navy attempted to fly the first plane to Hawaii in May 1925.

While military aircraft already were present in Hawaii in 1925, they had arrived by ship. The US Navy had developed three new seaplanes to attempt to fly to Hawaii, hopefully the first step in transpacific flights. No airplane of any type had ever flown over 1,500 miles before. To facilitate the trip, the Navy had stationed a series of ships between San Francisco and Hawaii. The ships would not only provide navigation aid but also serve as rescue vessels should the planes have to land at sea. Navigation was a tricky business in those days, particularly when it involved finding small islands in the vast Pacific. The planes flew a rhumb line route rather than the shorter great circle route; the rhumb line involved following a constant compass direction.

One seaplane was forced out of action at the start while the other two took off successfully from San Francisco Bay. They were so loaded with fuel that it took forty miles of flight for one of the planes to get above one hundred feet of elevation. One plane made it only about three hundred miles before being forced to land on the Pacific. The remaining plane ran out of fuel about three hundred miles from Hawaii. It was unable to locate the surface rescue vessel, and ships in the vicinity were unable to locate the plane.

The seaplane crew stripped fabric from its wings and constructed a sail and attempted to sail to Hawaii. The crew ran out of both food and water, but a chance heavy shower came along, and they were able to accumulate enough water to stay alive. Despite rigging a center-board, the seaplane could be sailed only a few degrees away from the direction of the wind. Finally, the seaplane sailed into the Kauai Channel and eventually was towed into Nawiliwili Harbor on Kauai. It was the first airplane to reach Hawaii from the mainland, but one could hardly say it flew there.

Flights from North America to Europe had already been made before the first successful flight to Hawaii was made, but even the poorest navigator could find Europe. Finding remote Honolulu was a real challenge!

Dr. G. says: In 1927 James Dole challenged pilots with a $25,000 prize for the first to fly from Oakland, California, to Honolulu. Two military planes, which had plans for the flight before the Dole prize was offered, became the first planes to fly from the mainland to Hawaii. Dole disqualified both: one landed at Wheeler Airfield, which was not in Honolulu at the time the flight was made. The other plane crash-landed on Molokai. Of the eleven planes that competed for the Dole prize, two actually made it to Honolulu. Ten lives were lost, and at least three planes were never found.

MINERALS AND MINES

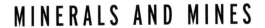

Question 141: Where is the largest gold mine in the world?

Question 142: Where is the largest silver mine in the world?

Question 143: What resource is derived from the Marcellus Shale?

Question 144: Where is the largest underground iron ore mine?

Question 145: Where is the principal iron ore deposit in the United States?

Gold is valuable primarily because it is scarce. If my calculations are right, all the gold ever found on earth could be placed in the infield of Yankee Stadium in a pile about sixty feet high. (Of course, the gold would fit in any baseball infield anywhere, but somehow it seems more appropriate to visualize it in Yankee Stadium.) Gold that almost certainly exists in native rocks is too heavy to appear on the surface of the earth (probably), so we need to thank gold-bearing asteroids that have collided with the earth for our supply. One asteroid in particular, one that struck near the present site of Johannesburg, South Africa, is responsible for more than 50 percent of all the gold in the world. Despite the past performance of South Africa, however, gold production has declined there in recent years.

Today the largest gold mine in the world is found in Indonesia, or, more specifically, on the half of the island of New Guinea that is Indonesian territory. It is called the Grasberg Mine, and it is less than two miles from the first major strike (now exhausted) that was discovered in 1936. The primary metal extracted from Grasberg is

Dr. G. says: I have been told by an amateur gold pros-
pector that the Witwatersrand lodes in South Africa were
highly frustrating to individual prospectors since the gold
there does not occur in the occasional lumps or nuggets of
nearly pure gold that so excites gold seekers but in an ore
that requires processing. Almost all gold requires processing, and most gold ore is low grade.

copper, and in addition to being the world's largest gold mine, it is
also the world's largest copper mine.

About half of all existing gold is found in jewelry. It does have industrial uses (for example, it is an excellent conductor of electricity),
but because of its cost, substitutes are used whenever possible. Until
quite recently, India was the largest consumer of gold. Wealth was
accumulated and stored in the form of bracelets and necklaces. Now,
however, the Chinese have become the largest consumers of gold.

Silver is more common than gold and of much lesser value. It, too,
has industrial uses and because of its lower price is more commonly
used, especially in electronics. In terms of economic geography,
silver may be more important than gold. In the middle of the sixteenth century, the Spanish found a huge supply of silver in what
is now Zacatecas, Mexico, and at almost the same time, they found
another enormous lode in Potosi, Bolivia. Silver, on the one hand,
was the metal that powered the Spanish Empire; on the other hand,
its availability set off rampant inflation in Spain.

Over time, Mexico has produced more silver than any other country, but currently the largest silver mine is the Cannington Mine in
Australia. In second place is the Fresnillo Mine in Zacatecas, Mexico. The production of these two mines is very close to equal, and
in any given year, a correct answer to the question could be either
mine. The third-largest producer is in San Cristobal, Bolivia.

Zacatecas Silver Mine

*   *   *

By enormous coincidence, Marcellus shale was the first rock I could identify. As a five-year-old, I considered a rock to be a rock. Any difference between one and another was simply a matter of size. My aunt and uncle owned what had been, in an earlier generation, a farm not far from Marcellus, New York. Their property was covered with flat-shaped rocks—shale. The Marcellus Shale can be found at varying depths in upstate New York, much of Pennsylvania, and parts of Virginia, West Virginia, and Ohio. There's an outcropping of the shale in Marcellus and other areas of central New York, which is how the formation was named (and where I first saw it).

The Marcellus Shale has proved to be a major source of natural gas, extractable through the technique known as hydraulic fracturing, or "fracking." The technology derives from attempts to extract additional oil from wells that were apparently exhausted. The ac-

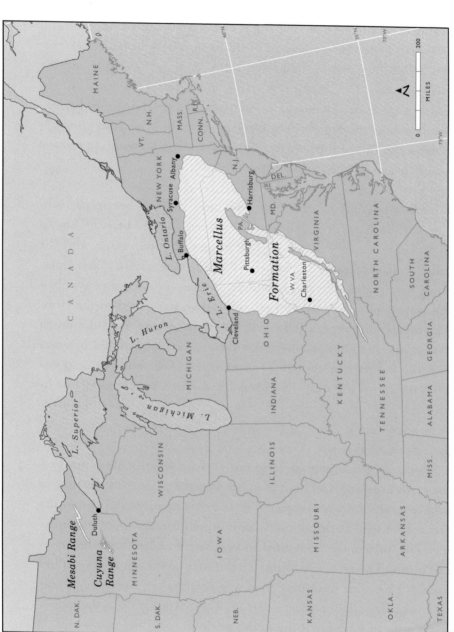

Marcellus Shale

tual process involves an amazing interplay between rocks, pressure, chemistry, and the application of fluids into bore holes. All extractive technology involves risks and actual damage to people and the environment. The question is: How much damage is acceptable in order to provide for energy needs? The United Kingdom has recently relaxed rules governing fracking, and the European Union is expected to follow suit. We can expect fracking, however, to remain a controversial issue for the foreseeable future.

I spent a portion of my childhood near an iron ore mine, now closed. The mine provided an object greatly sought by every boy in the town during the summer. The mine was a strip mine, and the vehicles that scraped and carried off the iron ore were called Euks, short for Euclid, the manufacturer. I have seen bigger tires than the Euks used, but never bigger tubes than were used in the tires. The tubes, too, were called Euks. When the tubes grew old enough and punctured enough, they were thrown out but coveted by every boy who was patient enough to patch them. The resulting craft was a battleship for use on Adirondack lakes. They were unassailable by ordinary tire tubes. I often wondered whether tire manufacturers knew what they'd done to the youth of America when they introduced the tubeless tire.

Most iron ore mines are strip mines. Iron is fairly ubiquitous on the earth's surface, and most iron ore with the potential to be turned into iron and steel is low grade. Low-grade ore does not justify the extra expense of building shafts and tunnels for underground mining. The Kirona iron ore mine in northern Sweden (Lapland) is an exception. The iron ore found on the surface is high grade, and as tunnels have been built over the years, the underground ore retains an unusually high percentage of iron. The Kirona mine is the largest underground iron ore mine in the world.

As testimony to the fact that iron is a common mineral, iron ore furnaces peppered colonial America. A number of towns in the Middle Atlantic region of the United States still bear the word "furnace" in their names, indicating their heritage as early iron producers. As the steel industry developed in the nineteenth century, it changed the landscape of the United States in some fundamental ways. Steel permitted the construction of skyscrapers, for example. Because steel production required iron ore, coal, and limestone as basic raw materials, industrial production tended to locate where these materials could be obtained most cheaply. Over time this meant that the industry tended to center in Pittsburgh—not because steelmakers planned it that way, but because Pittsburgh had such a cost advantage that it put a lot of other competing centers out of business.

The principal supplier of iron to Pittsburgh (and to other production centers) was a huge area of northern Minnesota that held the largest deposit of iron ore in the United States (and likely the world). The area is commonly referred to as the Mesabi Range, but in fact, the Mesabi Range is only about one-quarter of the iron-rich Minnesota Range.

From the late 1860s until the 1950s, the Minnesota Range produced a high-grade ore from a mineral called hematite. Although most of the iron was mined by strip mining, the hematite was valuable enough to justify underground mining. When the hematite ran out, the range essentially closed down in the 1950s. More recently, however, the demand for steel in China has been so great that portions of the range have reopened. Now, however, the ore is taconite, a lower-grade ore.

Dr. G. says: Some centers have always competed with Pittsburgh. Birmingham, Alabama, and Gary, Indiana, are notable examples. More recently, the demand for steel in the United States has been for a more specialized product where there is a cost advantage to being near the market rather than near the source of raw materials. Steel plants, for example, have opened in the Boston and New York areas.

LANDSCAPES OF FEAR

Question 146: What disease, whose pathogen was discovered by Howard Ricketts, was studied by the US Public Health Service in the Bitterroot Valley of Montana?

Question 147: What African parasitic disease, originally affecting only small pockets of isolated people, was spread by Arab slave traders and eventually killed millions?

Question 148: What was the name of the canal, never completed, that was intended to connect the Niagara River with Lake Ontario and became well known during President Carter's administration?

Question 149: What is the largest sand desert in the world?

Question 150: What is the driest area of Texas?

Fear has such a strong influence on us that it would seem certain that geographic theories and models would have to make some allowances for fear . . . but they don't. When I studied the movement of women to health clinics in Chile, I became convinced that fear was an influence on what clinic they chose or, indeed, whether they went to any clinic at all. All kinds of fears (if they can be broken down into categories) were present: fear of being molested en route, fear of getting lost, fear of dealing with strangers, fear of medicine. By ignoring the influence of fear, geographers may be overlooking some important questions.

I first began to see how people reacted differently to fear when I was a boy. When I was in third grade, our family moved from an urban environment to a small village in the Adirondacks of New York. Almost all my classmates at school had been born in the community, usually by home birth since the nearest hospital was four hours away and there was no doctor in the village. In the summer, a half-dozen of us would go for long treks in the woods. My companions would think nothing about walking over a six-inch-diameter log that spanned a hundred-foot fall to water and rocks below or to crawl into holes (which they incorrectly called "caves") that struck me as impossible to escape from unless there was an unknown wider spot somewhere. Because these things frightened me, I was left behind a lot at first. On the other hand, my friends were incredibly afraid of two things that fazed me not at all: ticks and blasting caps.

One boy told me that his mother (who was a Mohawk) insisted that he examine every inch of his body for ticks before he went to bed. She told him that a tick that did not sleep with you was not dangerous. If a tick was found, Dad was called, and he applied a lighted cigarette to the tick. I asked what ticks did, and the answer was "black measles." Years later I found out that "black measles" was a common name for Rocky Mountain spotted fever and that an infected tick may do no damage if removed within twelve to twenty-four hours. Blasting caps did not need to be explained further, since one of our group had already lost an eye to a cap—apparently a hazard in any mining community.

Dr. G. says: I would hardly be surprised if you thought the Adirondack Mountains were a surprising place for Rocky Mountain spotted fever. In fact, the disease, at least occasionally, is found in the eastern states except for northern New England. Please don't confuse this with Lyme disease, also spread by deer ticks but unknown until the mid-1970s. That, of course, doesn't mean that Lyme disease didn't exist before then, only that we weren't aware of it.

In the early twentieth century, the governor of Montana, according to one source, lost his wife and daughter to Rocky Mountain spotted fever. He made enough noise so that the US government set up a research camp (and later a major lab) in Montana to try to determine the vector of the disease. The Bitterroot Valley was the center of the research area. Howard Taylor Ricketts, a pathologist from Northwestern University, discovered that ticks were the vector. The pathogen was named after him (*Rickettsia*). It could not be determined whether the pathogen was a virus, a parasite, or a bacterium until the invention of the electron microscope. In fact, it is a bacterium, and in the 1940s (when my friend was still looking for ticks every night), it was discovered that the antibiotic tetracycline was an effective treatment.

Ironically, Ricketts went on to study typhus, another *Rickettsia* disease, which he caught and from which he died.

The chronicles of those who explored tropical Africa are more than a bit discouraging from a health standpoint. If the explorers weren't suffering from malaria, smallpox, or dysentery, they were being constantly annoyed and bitten by insects. Smallpox had a fatality rate of 20–60 percent of adult victims, dysentery in one form or another was probably the most common cause of death (and may still be, worldwide), and malaria, while less fatal, is debilitating. Having disposed of those ailments, let's get into a really bad one: sleeping sickness, or trypanosomiasis. Sleeping sickness comes in two forms; both are fatal if untreated. The acute form kills within months, while the more chronic form can take years. Between infection and death, victims often display psychotic symptoms and their sleep pattern is interrupted, so they sleep during the day and are awake at night.

The tsetse fly is the vector of the disease. Originally it was found only in isolated pockets of Africa, but the movement of Arab slave traders spread the disease widely, particularly in East Africa. Sleeping sickness, like malaria, is a parasitic disease and, although it is primarily spread from human to human (via the bite of the tsetse),

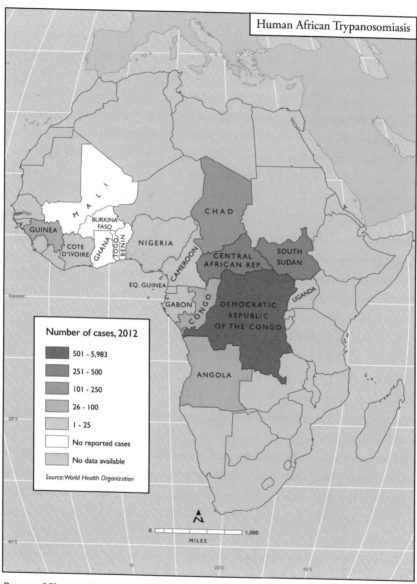

Range of Sleeping Sickness

it can also infect game and domestic animals. Treatment is available and quite effective if administered early. Nevertheless, tens of thousands die annually from it in Africa, and occasional outbreaks can kill hundreds of thousands.

Niagara Falls is an important tourist destination and, while no longer the honeymoon mecca of the past, it still attracts lots of visitors. At the same time, the falls is a huge barrier to navigation; were they not there, ships could use the Niagara River to travel from Lake Erie to Lake Ontario and hence to the Atlantic without the need for the Welland Canal or Erie Canal. In the 1890s, William T. Love envisioned a canal that would link the Niagara River with Lake Ontario. Only about a mile of the canal was ever dug. When it was abandoned, it filled with water. Children swam in it and skated on it in the winter. The City of Niagara Falls used it as a dump site for municipal waste in the 1920s.

In 1947, a chemical company was granted permission to dump its waste in the Love Canal. The company lined the canal bed with concrete and by the following year had become the sole user of the dump site. The chemicals were covered with twenty-five feet of soil, and by 1953, dumping ceased and grass and trees grew on top of the dump site.

The local school system decided to build not one but two schools on the site. The chemical company refused to sell, but the school board threatened eminent domain procedures, so the company gave the board the land for one dollar but with the written stipulation that it would not be liable for the chemicals buried in the old canal bed.

An entire community was built near the Love Canal site. Chemicals from the dump began to leak into basements and seep into lawns and gardens. Over time, outrage and panic grew, particularly as studies showed a higher incidence of birth defects in the area. No government agency seemed capable or interested in the plight of the canal neighborhood. As is often the case in dealing with hazardous areas, residents were deeply divided about what to do, if anything.

Eventually, President Jimmy Carter declared the Love Canal a disaster area, and people were evacuated and compensated for their losses. The so-called Superfund, a trust fund established by the US government to clean up areas of toxic waste, developed from the Love Canal disaster.

While scientists still debate the actual effect of the toxic waste on the people exposed to it, it is interesting that one authority alleged it was not the chemicals but the stress and panic individuals went through that caused damage to their health. While I think this allegation may be extreme, it underlines the importance of the "fear factor" in geographic theories and studies.

We associate deserts with sand, but the two don't necessarily go together. One of the driest areas in the world is Antarctica, but it has no sand to speak of. Although there is a good deal of sand in the Sahara, it is mostly gravel and rock. The Rub al Khali (or the Empty Quarter) is the world's largest sandy desert. It occupies more than two hundred thousand square miles, an area larger than Spain, and overlaps four countries: Saudi Arabia, Yemen, Oman, and the United Arab Emirates. Although the Empty Quarter is much, much smaller than the Sahara, it contains more than 50 percent of the volume of the Sahara's sand.

Before answering the book's last question directly, let's deal first with the theme of the chapter: fear. The Spanish explorer Coronado was the first European to cross what is now Texas. He was overwhelmed by a huge mesa that was palisaded on its edge with a rock formation that made it look like a fortification. Not surprisingly, Coronado named it the Llano Estacado, the "palisaded plain." Since then, almost everyone (including geographers) calls it the "staked plain," using the English cognate rather than the formal translation of *estacado*. I have heard at least a dozen explanations of why the plain is called what it is, all based on a misunderstanding of what Coronado meant.

Dr. G. says: According to a reliable source, a geographer stopped in a restaurant in a "wet" but rural area of Texas and asked for a glass of wine to go with his chicken-fried steak. Not wishing to be picky, he simply asked for a red. A rose was delivered. He said, "I asked for a red." "Oh," the waitress said, "you wanted a purple!"

Not only Coronado but anyone venturing into the area through most of the history of Texas would be justified in feeling fear. Not only was it an immense flat area with a lack of landmarks, but there was a lack of water sources, and, most importantly, it was the last refuge of the most powerful tribe to resist intrusion by the Spanish, the Mexicans, and the Americans: the Comanche. As I have pointed out in several of my writings, when you learn about a people who become militarily powerful, look to their weapons for the answer to their military success. In the case of the Comanches, it was the horse. They were legendary horsemen and so powerful militarily that they are likely the reason Mexico, at least initially, thought American settlement in Texas was a great idea.

The Llano Estacado is the driest area in Texas. When Prohibition ended in the United States, some counties in Texas kept it alive. Most of them (about forty in total) are in the Llano Estacado. Perhaps coincidentally (and perhaps not), the llano also has a significant concentration of churches and clergymen. Perhaps, having learned this for the first time, you, too, will be a bit fearful about crossing the llano!

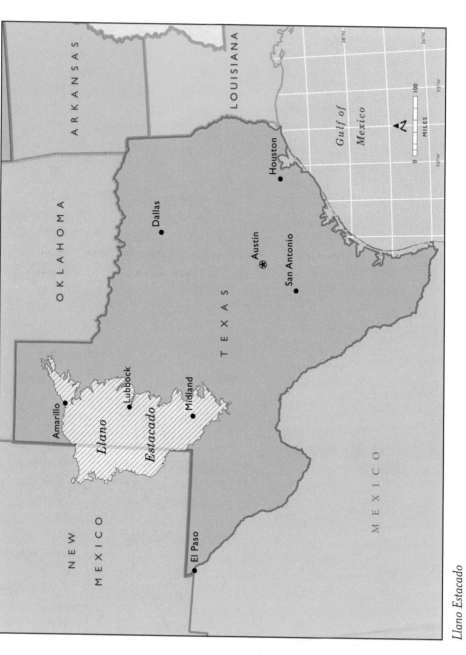

Llano Estacado

INDEX

Kea, 4; Mauna Loa, 4; Mont
Pelée, 4; most active (Kilauea),
1, 2–4; Mount Pichincha, 4;
Yellowstone, 1, 4
Volgograd, 47

War of 1812, 26, 28–29
Waterloo, battle of, 40, 44
Western Australia, 9; Freemantle
doctor, 9, 15; Perth, 15

Wilkes, Charles, 2; Ex Ex
Commander, 75, 78, 80
Wyoming, 1, 4

yellow fever, 85; "American
plague," 85–86; cause, 87
Yellow Fleet, 97, 100
yttrium, 109, 111

zocolo, 127, 133

ABOUT THE AUTHOR

Gary Fuller is professor emeritus of geography and population studies at the University of Hawaii. He is the author of the award-winning book *The Trivia Lover's Guide to the World: Geography for the Lost and Found* and was a winning contestant on the TV program *Jeopardy!* He lectures about geography on cruise ships and resides with his wife, Barbara, in Kailua, Hawaii.